The Inner World
of the Black
Juvenile Delinquent
Three Case Studies

The Inner World of the Black Juvenile Delinquent

Three Case Studies

Harrell B. Roberts
PRINCETON UNIVERSITY

LEA LAWRENCE ERLBAUM ASSOCIATES, PUBLISHERS

1987   Hillsdale, New Jersey   Hove and London

Lawrence Erlbaum Associates, Inc., Publishers
365 Broadway
Hillsdale, New Jersey 07642

Library of Congress Cataloging-in-Publication Data

Roberts, Harrell B.
   The inner world of the black juvenile delinquent.

   Based on the author's thesis (Ph.D.)—Rutgers, the
State University of New Jersey.
   Bibliography: p. 131
   Includes index.
   1. Juvenile delinquents—United States—Psychology—
Case studies.   2. Afro-American youth—Psychology—
Case studies.   I. Title.
HV9104.R62   1987   364.3'6'08996073   87-9006
ISBN 0-89859-895-8

Printed in the United States of America
10 9 8 7 6 5 4 3 2 1

To my wife, Ivory Sigler Roberts,
who has always believed in me
and my dreams

Contents

Acknowledgments

I wish first to acknowledge the pivotal contributions of the young men whose lives are the bases of the case studies. I am grateful to Jerome, Pete, and Sly for learning to trust me enough to be able to open themselves to my clinical scrutiny. It is hoped that their willingness to expose their inner individual worlds may enable other troubled adolescents to be better understood and therefore better served clinically.

The manuscript on which *The Inner World of the Black Juvenile Delinquent: Three Case Studies* is based was submitted as a dissertation to the Department of Psychology of Rutgers, The State University of New Jersey. I am indebted to Professor George Atwood, who served as my dissertation advisor, for his support, clinical expertise, and insightful contributions to the development of the manuscript. Princeton University granted me a leave of absence and financial support that were essential to finishing the book.

The quality of the text was greatly enhanced by the editorial guidance of Mrs. Mary Symons Strong. She possesses the rare ability to criticize without being destructive. Dr. Susan A. Darley read some portions of the manuscript and made valuable criticisms and suggestions. Mrs. Alice Bradshaw carefully typed and retyped sections of the many drafts and made helpful proposals for improvements.

I could never express fully my deepest sense of appreciation to my immediate and extended family for their understanding of my preoccupation with this project. My loving wife, Ivory, and my two daughters, Tammarah and Tracey, never failed to provide special support and encouragement during the darkest of times.

Foreword

The tragedy of the inner city black delinquent is a serious problem in our society. There are many reasons for this state of affairs, and a host of solutions are required.

The first step toward a solution is understanding the troubled minds of these youngsters. Because their actions cause anger in so many around them, family, friends, and observers are often unwilling to provide help.

The social dynamics, psychology, and pathology of the inner city are similar to those described by Kenneth Clark in *Dark Ghetto.* Describing delinquency, he states:

> The possibility that a young person may act out his frustration in ways inconvenient to more priveledged persons outside of the ghetto—through thefts to support the drug habit, through vandalisms and muggings in subways and buses, through the stoning of trains—arouses retaliatory concern from the larger threatened society. The Negro delinquent, therefore, calls attention to the quiet pathology of the ghetto which he only indirectly reflects. In a curious way the delinquent's behavior is healthy; for, at the least, it asserts that he still has sufficient strength to rebel and has not yet given in to defeat. (p. 88)

It is unusual to consider destructive and violent behavior in the context of health. However, it becomes inexplicable when the alternative can be seen as death. Dr. Roberts' book provides an understanding and insight into the lives of three black adolescents, each of whom seeks an identity of importance and value in the struggle against a psychic death.

The Inner World of the Black Juvenile Delinquent: Three Case Studies is a penetrating analysis achieved with objectivity, sensitivity, and clarity. The author offers a rationale for hope. Early intervention, as an aid in rebuilding the intimate fabric of a positive identity, is essential.

Duncan E. Walton
Rutgers University

1

Introduction: Perspectives on Black Delinquent Behavior

The case studies of the three black adolescents that are presented in this book were undertaken as a way of gaining a better understanding of how each boy's psychological development contributed to his delinquent behavior. Sharing similar backgrounds of extreme poverty and ghetto life, each one of these young men had committed virtually the same series of increasingly serious infractions of the law that eventually had led to arrest and incarceration in a state facility for juvenile offenders. Although they appeared to have traveled the same road to jail, in fact each boy had followed his own circuitous route, psychologically speaking, through the thorny byways of developmental experiences. Each youth in his own special way and at a particular stage of growth encountered problems in dealing with the significant adults in his life—a mother who was rearing him and a father who was absent most of his life. It is in the context of their unique psychological histories that the meaning and motivation for their delinquent behavior have been examined.

THE SOCIOCULTURAL CONTEXT AND THE PSYCHODYNAMICS OF BLACK DELINQUENTS

It is impossible to understand the delinquent behavior of inner-city black boys without considering the variety of ways the social conditions of the ghetto impinge on the lives of its population. For a child growing up in these circumstances, the space beyond the family living quarters is physically and psychologically threatening, especially during the boy's adolescence and early adulthood. In poor black neighborhoods the reality of life is the fact of omnipresent danger to the residents. All the denizens of the ghettos of our large and small cities are less safe than people living elsewhere. Blacks suffer

1

more from attack on life, limb, and property than any other group. Although blacks comprise approximately 12% of the U.S. population, they constitute 41% of the persons meeting death by homicide. Most of these victims are males between the ages of 15 and 44, with the younger males being at particularly high risk. In contrast, whites make up 56% of the homicide victims although having a population about eight times larger than the number of Black Americans (Federal Bureau of Investigation, 1985). Of the 7,290 males murdered in 1984, 3,607 or approximately 50% were black. A homicide death rate nine times higher than that for whites and appearing among the ten leading causes for death for nonwhite males reflects the overt terror in the ghetto.

In addition to being at higher risk for meeting a violent death, Black Americans are the most frequent targets of other kinds of serious violent crime. Individual blacks are nearly twice as likely as whites to be robbed, raped, assaulted, burglarized, and have their cars stolen. Within the black community it is the poorer, younger, and males members of the population who are the most likely victims. According to the National Crime Survey Report (1983), a composite portrait of the most likely object of serious violence is a person 16 to 19 years old, male, black, unemployed, and from a family with less than a $3,000 annual income.

Although poor Black Americans are vulnerable to a high volume of crime, at the same time they report that they can not rely on the police for protection. Residents of black communities describe the police as ineffectual in law enforcement and unfair, abrasive, and violent towards them without justification (President's Crime Commission, 1967). Black adolescents in particular view the police as a set of antagonists who abuse their powers without hesitation. Their perception of police harassment may well be accurate. Studies have shown that black males are stopped more often than whites by police where they lack any sort of evidence that an offense has been committed and that black youth are arrested more often than whites for similar offenses. In many poor communities, the police are seen as "an occupying force, an army" (Hearings, Criminal Justice Subcommittee, House Judiciary Committee, 1984). In testimony at congressional hearings on police brutality blacks stated that they were afraid to call the police when they were victims of crime because such a call would place them in jeopardy: "Calling a police officer can be hazardous to your health. It can result in death, serious physical injury, and almost certain spiritual abuse of your person and your dignity."

Although the facts just indicated show how much at risk black youth are on a daily basis, black lower class parents do not need this statistical information to realize that they must do all in their power to protect their male children from potential trouble. Danger to themselves and their families is always present. The danger to black youth is of two kinds, and the parents are well aware of this. Not only may their sons be victims of crime, but they may also be easily involved in committing crimes. Crime is in the street, and the children are exposed to it constantly. In fact, youngsters can and do learn to pilfer, snatch pocketbooks, vandalize property, and steal from other persons at an early age. Parents know that these types of offenses lay the groundwork for more serious acts and for police records. They are acquainted with young people who have started out this way and ended up in correctional facilities for youth and eventually in penitentiaries. This knowledge that their sons possess a greater chance than any other group in this country of meeting and having their lives terminated by violence must cause such parents to act in a certain protective manner toward their male children. Such parental behavior would be reality oriented, not based on fantasy nor on neurotic needs.

The psychodynamic development of a black delinquent reared in a ghetto neighborhood is embedded in his experience within a family unit and with other individuals and groups who in turn play out their existence in the same social context. When attempting to analyze some possible connections between the antisocial behavior of an individual youngster and his psychodynamics the boy cannot be extracted from this social context. Nor is it possible to appreciate the nature and source of his delinquent behavior without grasping the manner in which the social, economic, and cultural forces operate to influence the psychological worlds of his parents, siblings, friends, and the other adults who come into his life, each of whom is affected by a shared environment and in turn influences the growing child by interacting with him. As the youngster lives among these people in their common ghetto neighborhood, the relationships with the significant others in his life bend and shape his psychological world, turning it in certain directions, preparing the youngster—sometimes even propelling him—to engage in acts that the mainstream society regards as antisocial and illegal.

There is no doubt that a ghetto child grows up in a social context that may be conducive to antisocial behavior. A society can only elicit voluntary compliance with its standards of conduct when its members think the rules of behavior are legitimate and basically fair and beneficial to them. On the other hand, when the system is perceived by them as unjust, they may either rebel against it or accommodate to their inferior status grudgingly, taking a stance of passive resistance or apathy. For black youth reared in the underclass and confined to the poverty, social disorganization, and virtual hopelessness of life in the ghetto, the objective conditions of their surroundings and prospects do not encourage a belief in the equity or justice of the system. These beliefs and feelings may have a great impact on them from a very early age because the adults around them also carry the injuries inflicted on them by a dehumanizing social order.

Beyond Social Determinism

Some argue, and with good reason, that the delinquency of lower class youth can be attributed entirely to the oppressive social conditions in which black slum dwellers live. In fact, it is suggested that no purpose is served by probing into the psychological makeup of these boys because being poor and black in America suffices as an explanation for their delinquencies.

In addition, according to this point of view, the mere fact of raising questions about the connection between the psychological world of the youngster and his antisocial behavior foreshadows a predictable set of negative judgments about the boy's responsibility for his own acts. Implicit in such judgments, it is suggested, is a shift of the blame for his conduct from its proper source in the unjust social order onto the individual delinquent, his parents, the black community, and/or the so-called culture of poverty. Predictably, the child is diagnosed as emotionally ill and often given the label of psychopath instead of placing the onus for his antisocial behavior on the degrading environment where it rightly belongs. Finally, the claim is made that it is the aggressive, violent, and immoral child who is sick, forgetting about the society that is pathological.

These fears are justifiably voiced, but they do not cancel out the need for a more adequate explanation of the genesis of delinquent behavior. The position of the social determinist—that the ghetto is a breeding ground for crime—fails to account for the wide variation of individual responses to the social conditions in the ghetto. In fact, it does not give sufficient credit to the capacities of ghetto residents to create personal stability in the midst of social chaos. Although an environment makes a palpable imprint on its residents, it is still not capable of turning out clones. The determinist argument implies a one-to-one correlation between social conditions and delinquency, one that simply does not exist. Only a small percentage of ghetto youth are arrested and jailed for delinquency, although many others have one-time brushes with the law during adolescence. Moreover, there are many middle-class youth who come from distinctly favorable backgrounds, but also commit antisocial acts (often considered "just pranks") and usually avoid being punished, almost never going to jail.

Another argument of the social determinists is that ghetto youngsters are compelled to steal as a means of survival. Actually there is no evidence to support this notion. Although the pilfering, shoplifting, and breaking and entering may in many instances be related to not having enough money to buy the things a youngster desires to own, the case can rarely be made that these acts are engaged in out of necessity for physical survival.

Another unsupportable claim of the social determinist is that most of the members of the ghetto community consider delinquent activities normal and acceptable conduct and actually expect their sons and husbands to engage in crime. Although it is true that people living in poverty have much less investment in the social order than other segments of the population, at the same time it has been found in surveys of attitudes of ghetto adults that a great majority subscribe to the same beliefs in law and order shared by the rest of the society. Mainstream norms of lawful conduct are accepted and upheld as ultimately valid even though it is also recognized that it is often difficult to abide by them under the stressful circumstances ghetto residents are faced with.

Black parents do not condone delinquent behavior by their children. This is true despite the fact that they struggle against enormous odds to provide even minimum levels of subsistence for their children. Although they cope with many social and economic conditions that threaten daily to undermine their best efforts to lead decent, satisfactory lives—low-paying jobs, high levels of unemployment, welfare dependency, racism and racial discrimination, vermin and rat infested run-down neighborhood, delapidated, dangerous housing, deteriorating public services, poor schools, and crime, the majority of families almost miraculously keep their children out of the serious kinds of trouble that lead to frequent arrest and eventual imprisonment. Under the given circumstances what is more remarkable is that the amount of deviancy from the social norms and the level of rebellion against their discouraging lot do not result in even more widespread antisocial behavior by black youngsters.

Social Stress and Psychological Functioning

The fact is that the social environment of the ghetto has highly differential effects on the personal lives of its residents. It is both simplistic and inaccurate to lump all black slum dwellers into a monolithic heap. As with every human being, each person in an inner-city neighborhood acquires his own world through his personal experiences, while sharing a social context with others. As the child grows, his experiences are largely mediated through those who tend him as a baby and young child and interact with him later as an adolescent, young man, and adult. Of course, he also experiences the social conditions of his immediate neighborhood and school directly and the culture of the larger society through the media.

What is crucial in making the connection between the delinquent boy's social environment and his psychodynamic development is that all the members of the social network who have touched his life significantly have been influenced throughout their lives by the stressful conditions of ghetto life. In other words, this environment not only has a direct influence on the boy as he walks the streets, but it has affected the daily patterns of life and indeed the personalities of people closest to him. Their responses to the baleful conditions leave their mark, whether good or bad, on the psychodynamic development of the young child and growing youth. Those earliest interactions with the mother, for example, become the emotional foundations on which the child's psychological life is built. Because the mothers are frequently under duress themselves, they may be experienced as agents of psychological deprivation by their children. On the other hand, other mothers who have similarly difficult life situations are experienced by their children as nurturing, but not to the extent deemed adequate by the child. It is expected that the boys' delinquent behavior will reflect this range of early developmental experiences. Some will have considerable difficulty in their psychological growth whereas others will enjoy a less traumatic course of development.

The social context in which the residents of the ghetto live out their lives puts an enormous degree of social pressure on both the individual and the community, creating chronic tensions that can be the seedbed for a variety of responses indicating personal stress. Besides the economic deprivation, racism imposes an added burden on the psychological adaptation of blacks by making direct assaults on the sense of self and self-respect of Black Americans.

Analyzing the psychodynamics of the delinquent behavior of ghetto youth does not ignore the oppressive social conditions in which they grow up. On the contrary, the idea of such a conceptualization of the problem is to take the social context of delinquency more fully into account by attempting to specify the links between the effects of the context on the psychodynamics of youthful offenders and their antisocial behavior. The relationships among these elements are complex ones and highly individualized for each boy. Consequently the interactions of the sociocultural environment of the ghetto with the significant others in a boy's life will vary greatly in their influences on his psychodynamics and his behavior.

The stresses on the black population of living in a dehumanizing social system are many and take their toll in various ways. Considering the extent of the pressures on them, however, Black Americans have remarkably good mental health. The means of coping with their sense of discouragement, failure, and frustration, particularly as experienced by low-status blacks, are found with various degrees of success. When things become overwhelming, some resort to the use of alcohol, drugs, whereas others are faced with various levels of psychological difficulties. In the case of many ghetto youth, their so-called delinquent behavior may be seen as attempts to push away the sadness, pathology, and hate that encroaches on them. Their delinquent acts may be their way of establishing a sense of self-respect and efficacy—ways of feeling less victimized by the society and by their mothers and fathers who denied them the full measure of caring and the material goods that were supposed to make them feel good about themselves.

JUVENILE DELINQUENCY: RESEARCH PERSPECTIVES

As a way of laying the groundwork for understanding the psychological world of the lower class black delinquent boy, pertinent studies of delinquency are presented under the following general headings: (1) social and cultural interpretations of delinquency; (2) psychological perspectives on the personalities of delinquents; and (3) psychoanalytic-clinical approaches to the understanding of the delinquent.

Social and Cultural Interpretations

It was the sociologists who undertook to relate delinquency to the social structure, minority and ethnic status, economic and class standing, and the various cultural traditions of American society. In doing this they used census data and police records to create statistical indices for the rates of delinquency and crime in the population. Being lower class and residing in a slum area, it was found, put youth at greater risk of having a police record in the central cores of major American cities in which the succeeding waves of immigrants lived, including black migrants from the South. Deteriorated neighborhoods, poor housing, poverty, and unemployment were correlated with high-delinquency rates and frequently seen as the causes of crime and delinquency. In other words, the pressures of the environment were regarded as the principal influences contributing to delinquency.

The ideas of Merton (1938, 1957) about the genesis of various forms of nonconforming behavior provided a theoretical framework for explaining delinquency that had been lacking in the purely correlational empirical approach of the earlier studies. Making a distinction between the goals of a society and the means offered to its citizens for achieving them, Merton argued that the goal of success (usually monetary) had been extolled in the United States without the equivalent opportunity for everyone to achieve success legally. Crime and delinquency rates would differ according to whether a person could achieve the goal of success through legitimate means or had to use illegal ones. Those in lower socioeconomic positions who did not have access to the legitimate means of making money, for example, would predictably take the illegitimate path to the goals the society had inculcated in them.

Over the years Merton's ideas have stimulated research to test various implications of his notions about why certain categories of people would not abide by the standards and laws of a society. In the course of time the ideas were criticized, modified, and extended. Of course, one of the weaknesses of the theory was that it failed to explain why not all lower class youth committed delinquent acts in their pursuit of the success goal (Reckless & Dinitz, 1967).

Asking whether access to illegal means for acquiring material goods (purse snatching, car stealing, techniques for breaking and entering) were not also distributed differentially throughout society, Cloward (1959) pointed out that some lower class boys have better opportunities to learn ways of committing delinquent acts than others. Cohen (1955) also challenged the idea that all lower class boys accepted the standards of conventional society. In their gangs they took part in a delinquent subculture that denied the goals of middle-class respectability and put a premium on flouting its rules by committing negativistic and malicious acts of vandalism and theft. Elaborating on this further, Cloward and Ohlin (1960) agreed that there was a kind of "reaction formation" to American values by lower class youth who participated in one of three different subcultures of delinquency: one organized around fighting and attacks on rival gangs, another around theft, and a third around drugs and other escapist activities.

Developing the theme that there were cultural norms supporting illegal activities, some investigators have suggested that there were values in lower class culture that made it, in the words of Miller (1958), a "generating milieu" for delinquency and crime. In inner-city neighborhoods, where much stock is put on toughness, smartness, excitement, and resistance to authority, boys were apt to become involved in unlawful activities such as fighting and theft. Although these interpretations did not claim that lower class values actually demanded violations of the law, they did offer an explanation of how such values might help create conditions where delinquent acts were more likely to occur and even be considered normal behavior. Put another way, there were crimogenic influences operating in American society.

Psychological Perspectives

In contrast with the social and cultural perspectives of sociologists, psychologists have not been satisfied with such general, global explanations of delinquency. They wanted to know the personal psychological problems of delinquent youth that turned a minority of them in the direction of committing delinquencies on a steady basis although the majority did not. The thrust of the research from a psychological perspective has been on the creation of typologies of interaction (Bandura & Walters, 1959), of behavior patterns and backgrounds (Hewitt & Jenkins, 1947), and on other problems using questionnaires and scales to determine the personality differences between delinquents and nondelinquents. However, it has generally turned out to be difficult to pinpoint readily identifiable delinquent types that were distinguishable from one another (Jenkins & Glickman, 1947).

Gough, Peterson, Quay and their associates have been involved in a long-term effort to create instruments for measuring the personality dimensions of delinquents and nondelinquents. They found that delinquents were less adequate in their role-taking ability (Gough & Peterson, 1952) and less expressive of their attitudes and feelings (Quay & Peterson, 1958). A factor analysis of responses to a questionnaire by 100 white delinquent and nondelinquent boys matched for age and community of residence yielded four personality factors that separated the two groups (Peterson, Quay, & Cameron, 1959). Those who were delinquent had at least one of the following clusters of qualities: (1) the psychopathy factor—the boys affirmed and endorsed rebellious behavior; (2) the neuroticism factor—the boys admitted tension, guilt, and remorse; (3) a factor that indicated that the boy came from a home in which there was dissension in the family and also that he had conflicts with school personnel; and (4) an inadequacy factor—the boy showed a general inability to cope with a complex world.

Administering the same questionnaire plus selected items from the MMPI and the Kvarceus KD Proneness Scale, Peterson, Quay, and Tiffany (1961) found the psychopathy and neuroticism factors present in the delinquents. A Q-sort method used by Tiffany, Peterson, and Quay (1961) in another study yielded the same four personality dimensions, but the subjects did not coalesce into types. Instead they distributed themselves differentially and normally over the four dimensions. The investigators came to the conclusion that there were no clear trends for the subjects to load highly on any one factor:

> These delinquents did not "naturally" group themselves into distinct types . . . trait analyses seem to offer promise, but it must be recognized that these define dimensions of behavior rather than types of people and that the actual existence of distinct, unitary groups within the delinquent population have not yet been demonstrated. (p. 24)

This should not be a surprising conclusion because it would be safe to say that a large segment of the adolescents who are not delinquent might also describe themselves in terms of one or more of these factors and distribute themselves normally over the four dimensions of being rebellious against parental control, having some difficulties at home and at school, admitting guilt, remorse, and tensions, and, finally, feeling some inadequacy in dealing with the complex world—altogether recognizable experiences of all adolescents.

In any case it would be unlikely that much insight into a phenomenon as complex as delinquent behavior could be secured on the basis of the administration of instruments on a one-shot approach, as convenient and efficient a mode of studying delinquency as that may be. There is also a problem in such self-descriptions on a one-time questionnaire in that the delinquent boys being studied might have a personal investment in proving to outsiders such as researchers that they are really tough, defiant, and/or "crazy."

In a 5-year study of disturbed juvenile delinquents who had committed serious offenses and been sent by the courts to a maximum security hospital, Offer, Marohn, and Ostrov (1979) carried on in-depth interviews, administered a series of rating scales and finally factor analyzed the data secured from 55 boys and girls, 17 of whom were black. Their analysis produced four dimensions, each of which could be typified by a particular kind of delinquent: (1) the impulsive; (2) the narcissistic; (3) the depressed borderline; and (4) the empty borderline. In creating these subtypes of disturbed delinquents, each subject was observed, interviewed, and rated on a wide array of instruments over a 13-week period. The duration of the observation was an advance over the single-session contacts of many research designs and was made possible, of course, by the subjects' forced confinement. Although their study was aimed at preserving the individuality of the subjects through the study of the psychological life of each patient, in the end the individual was lost in a flood of psychological tests and resultant typologies that washed away the inner psychological world of the individual. Typologies necessarily contravene the spirit of intensive focus on the individuals no matter how long or intensive the interaction with the person being studied may have been.

Psychoanalytic-Clinical Approaches

Working in the psychoanalytic tradition, clinicians focused their attention on the psychodynamics of the individual offender. Well known for their pioneering case studies comparing delinquents with their nondelinquent siblings, Healy and Bronner (1926, 1936) portrayed delinquents as suffering from severe psychopathologies. Such interpretations of delinquent behavior were unfortunately applied to the whole population of offenders by other researchers proposing psychodynamic explanations of delinquency (Grossbard, 1962; Johnson, 1949; Johnson & Szurek, 1952). The notion that every delinquent had a grossly deviant character structure died hard in this tradition.

On the positive side, the psychoanalytic tradition contributed a deeply empathic commitment to the study of the delinquent as an individual. It was Aichhorn, a disciple of Freud and often regarded as the father of the psychoanalytic understanding of delinquent youngsters, whose compelling book on *Wayward Youth* (1935) brought attention to the personal problems of the Viennese adolescents in trouble with the law, those whom he called "dissocial youth." The outward characteristics of their delinquent behavior, in his view, were less important to understand than the psychic mechanisms that motivated their "dissocial behavior." On the basis of his detailed case studies of these boys, Aichhorn showed that many of them had experienced grave difficulties during their early child rearing and brought the pathological interaction patterns created at that time into their subsequent relationships. Aichhorn (1935) found that "the dissocial child shows regularly a love life that has been disturbed in early childhood by a lack of affection or an undue amount of affection" (p. 119). The achievement of adequate social adjustment rested on particular conditions; these included satisfactory constitutional endowment and early love relationships with suitable boundaries. "The child develops normally and assumes his proper place in society if he can cultivate in the nursery such relationships as can favourably be carried over into school and from there into the ever-broadening world around him. . . . People whose early adjustments follow such normal course have no difficulties of forming libidinal object relationships which are considered normal by society." In contrast, the delinquent was marked by "his inability to regulate his conscious and unconscious libidinal strivings and to confine his libidinal expectations within normal bounds" (Aichhorn, 1935: 119-20). For Aichhorn, these abnormal libidinal ties were the conditions from which delinquency developed.

To help the incarcerated child return to society one must first understand the psychodynamics underlying his "dissocial behavior" and possibly be the first person to provide him with individual caring. Aichhorn (1935) wrote:

> The great majority of children in need of retraining come into conflict with society because of an unsatisfied need for tenderness and love in their childhood. We therefore find in them a proportionately increased thirst for pleasure and for primitive forms of instinctual gratification. They lack inhibitions and they have a strong, though distorted, craving for affection. If the delinquency is to be cured rather than repressed, we must meet these needs even though at first this seems futile to so-called "understanding people. (p. 120)

The issue of understanding the individual psychodynamics of each youngster was also highlighted in a psychoanalytic classic of the 1950s, *Children Who Hate* by Redl and Wineman (1951). They make the point that in treating delinquent children one must truly understand the "clinical concept" that is particular to everyone of these young people.

> The *"clinical concept"* of delinquency is not in contradiction with the cultural or legal one but should be considered as an attempt to specify and supplement where the others left off. However, it is of great relevance, indeed, for the educator and clinician. We primarily have in mind the sharp difference we are forced to make between the assessment of the *delinquent behavior* involved in a case and the question of the *basis* on which such behavior occurred. . . . Just what variety of personality disturbances may be referred to when we make a statement that the youngster's stealing was on a "delinquent basis" may vary from case to case. (pp. 142-143)

But one has to go even beyond the clinical question to fully understand these children. A psychoanalytic insight of the 1970s offered by Winnicott (1973) was that the youngster whose behavior has been labeled delinquent may well be trying to make a statement that was usually not heard by legal, judicial, penal, and many clinical personnel. For him, delinquent acts on the part of adolescents should be viewed as an S.O.S., a distress signal, and may also serve to be a sign of hope. In his address to British juvenile officers he said it was a mistake to relate juvenile delinquent behavior to general conditions such as impoverishment, inferior housing, broken families, parental deviance, and social decay. More importantly, Winnicott (1973) stated that "in every case that comes your way, there was a beginning and at the beginning there was an illness, and a boy or girl became a deprived child. In other words there is a sense in what once happened although by the time that each individual comes into your care the sense has usually become lost" (pp. 364–365).

For Winnicott it was crucial to give a youngster who has become involved with committing delinquent acts an opportunity to talk about himself. In the unique conditions of psychotherapy a youngster is capable of remembering a traumatic experience of deprivation. Winnicott (1973) stated:

> A child who has been deprived . . . has first suffered unthinkable anxiety. . . . Then for some reason or other hope begins to appear, and this means that the child, *without being conscious of what's going on* (emphasis mine), begins to have the urge to get back behind the moment of deprivation and so to undo the fear of the unthinkable anxiety or confusion. . . . Whatever conditions give a child a certain degree of new hope, then the antisocial tendency becomes difficult. (p. 366)

Based on their work with lower class, urban black and Puerto Rican delinquents who were committed to the Wiltwyck School for Boys, Minuchin and his associates developed a treatment approach that became known as the structural method of family therapy (Minuchin et al., 1967). Their view was that delinquent behavior was reflective of a family system being in some form of disarray. According to their observations, delinquents were more likely to come from "disorganized, pathological families" than from the more stable families living under similar conditions of poverty and racism. These disorganized, pathological families were distinguished from the stable ones by the higher incidence of crime, drug addiction, alcoholism, instability, disease, and joblessness. The major structural features of the troubled families were passive, powerless mothers who relinquished executive control to the children, absent fathers, and parental children who attempted to act as adults in the absence of parental control. These researchers saw the task of family therapy with such a population as (1) helping the families by restoring executive functioning to the head of the family, (2) increasing effective communication between parents and children, and (3) modifying the sibling subsystem of parenting. According to the structuralists, it was the family dynamics that not only had generated the delinquent behavior but also served to maintain it (Minuchin & Fishman, 1981).

Minuchin's rationale for developing the structural method of family therapy was a radical departure from his individually oriented psychoanalytic training. This change of approach derived from his belief that lower class persons, blacks among others, could not benefit from dynamic, one-to-one, introspective, talking psychotherapy, a judgment shared by many others (Bernstein, 1964; Bredemeier, 1964; Gans, 1963; Gordon, 1965; Hunter, 1964; McMahon, 1964; Visotsky, 1963). This widely accepted view was captured in a statement made by Minuchin et al. (1967) in their book, *Families of the Slums:* "The low socioeconomic population became known as an 'unreachable' group because individual psychotherapy traditionally stressed a permissive environment, a nondirective approach, and a free-association atmosphere and relied on the patient's remembering past events and exploring affect—skills which are underdeveloped in this population" (p. 35).

THE STUDY OF BLACK DELINQUENTS

Seldom have the lives of individual black juvenile delinquents been scrutinized with sufficient intensity to obtain a comprehensive understanding of what lies behind their antisocial behavior. Most of these young offenders—who make up the largest proportion of the inmate population in the jails for juveniles in the United States—would not be classified as either severely emotionally disturbed or organically impaired. However, it is highly likely that many of them have experienced some serious emotional trauma during their formative years. In the study of black delinquents reported in the subsequent chapters there was an attempt to discover whether their delinquent behavior was in some way linked to serious difficulties in their early histories.

About the Study

The method chosen for studying the delinquent youngster's psychological development was that of the intensive psychobiographical case study. It has been demonstrated that the case study method of psychological investigation has been a valuable tool for further understanding personality (Allport, 1961; Murray, 1938; White, 1952, 1953). The particular theoretical framework adopted was "psychoanalytic phenomenology" (Stolorow & Atwood, 1979) that has consisted of looking at the many facets and intricacies of the human personality from the standpoint of the individual to indicate in his own unique way how he perceived the world and his place in the world. This orientation assumed that unconscious, as well as conscious experiences—how one relates to oneself, the important others in one's life, and the larger world—could be organized in terms of themes particular to each person. The assumption was that the organizing themes of a person's life were the result of important developmental experiences and could best be understood by studying the person's style of interacting with the larger world. Psychoanalytic phenomenology differed from other theories of personality in that it did not aim at providing a theory concerning the nature of the personality considered as an "objective entity." Instead it provided a methodological framework of interpretive principles to guide the study of meaning in human behavior and experience.

Whereas the case study method has occupied a major place in clinical research dating back to Breuer and Freud, it has not been as popular within academic research. Academic research has at its core the experimental-deductive method in which specifically prestated hypotheses were tested, utilizing variables that were free of the phenomenological-historical contexts of specific persons. In contrast, the case study method supposed that testing of hypotheses—having pertinence for a large group of subjects—could be attempted only after a significant amount of groundwork had been established by the of individual subjects (McWilliams, 1976). Stolorow and Atwood (1979) have emphasized that the case study approach "is inherently a personalistic and phenomenological enterprise. . . . It repeatedly raises the interpretative question, what is the experiential and life historical context within which various regions of the person's behavior have meaning?" (p. 40).

The validity of the case study method should be appreciated in terms of its particular rationale and purpose. Neither a "strategy of proof" nor an attempt to present "final truths and incontrovertible general principles regarding human personality," it was a means of proceeding with the purpose of generating "significant theoretical ideas" and suggesting "promising lines of research through intensive sustained confrontation with the empirical complexity and idiosyncrasy of actual persons" (Stolorow & Atwood, 1979, p. 41).

The current study in many ways followed closely the procedures used by White (1952) in his study of three adults and those of Diller (1979) in her investigation of three dancers. White (1952) wrote that his method of personality research was "designed to reveal the multiplicity of influences surrounding them (persons being studied) (and) their effect on their environment" (p. 25). Both White and Diller made use of projective tests, observations, and interviews to allow their subjects to express their hopes, fears, self-estimates, dreams of the future, and aspirations. Although this method has not been the only means of attempting to study personality, the case study method, according to White (1952), has allowed a researcher to learn most completely a person's "ego, self, and those other integrations that are so important in giving overall form and direction to life" (p. 99).

The black adolescents who became the subjects of the three case studies were selected with the assistance of the staff of a state facility for juvenile offenders with histories of recidivism. A boy was considered appropriate as a subject if he (1) voiced difficulty with his mother's efforts to discipline and control him, (2) expressed a desire not to return home upon being paroled, (3) had committed crimes against women, and (4) was willing to talk about himself.[1] The three young men were similar in their backgrounds and probably typical of a majority of the inmate population in most of their demographic characteristics—each was from lower class socioeconomic circumstances, did not have his father as part of the family, and had a history of numerous prior offenses.

Initially information about each boy was gathered with the use of an 18-item checklist that included questions about his personal history, his relationships with his primary others, his criminal acts, and his interactions with the larger world (see Appendix A). Subsequent interviews—which were usually conducted on a weekly basis and lasted over a period of from 4 to 12 months for each of the subjects—were aimed at understanding the subjective reports given by a boy about his feelings, thoughts, memories, and experiences that were seen as being important to him and that might influence his current behavior.[2] Such a procedure allowed the subject to indicate to the researcher how he happened to view the world and himself within the world. The framework that the interviews were built around included the subject's (1) personal background, (2) family background, (3) educational history, (4) mother–son interactions, (5) separation issues, (6) feelings about himself, (7) concepts of manliness, (8) types and nature of interactions with women, (9) friendships, (10) sexual experiences, (11) understanding of his deviant behavior, and (12) current and previous aspirations. The personal experience of each of the delinquent youngsters was intensely investigated to gain a multifaceted understanding of his psychodynamics. Such psychological understanding provided for a better comprehension of the individualized function of delinquency and violence for each boy and allowed for an assessment of the salience of antisocial behavior in the life of each one of the adolescents.

In addition to the intensive interviews, each boy was given the following projective tests: the Thematic Apperception Test (TAT), the Draw-A-Person (DAP), and the Holsapple–Miale Sentence Completion Test (SCT). The TAT cards, which were selected to correspond to personal situations likely to be significant to the subjects, consisted of: 1, 3BM, 4, 5, 6BM, 7BM, 8BM, 9BM, 12M, 13MF, 14, 15, 16, 17BM, 18BM, 18GF, and 20 (see Appendix B for descriptions of TAT cards). The 73 items of the Holsapple–Miale Sentence Completion Test were read to each youngster for his response. For the

---

[1]These criteria were selected as part of an earlier pilot study that dealt with the role of maternal domination in male juvenile delinquency. These characteristics of the subjects of the earlier study, however, in no way make the subjects unrepresentative of black delinquents in general. Preliminary interviews lasting between 30 and 45 minutes were conducted initially with five boys, and of these, three were selected for the case studies.

[2]The interviews were conducted in a manner modeled after Murray (1938) and Diller (1979) who used life history inquiries to further understand their subjects' characters.

Draw-A-Person test, each boy was asked by the researcher to draw a figure. After the first figure was drawn, the subject was asked to draw a person of the opposite sex. After these drawings were finished, the adolescent was asked to describe each one of the figures in the order in which they were drawn. The oral responses to the tests were tape recorded, and excerpts from these recordings were included in the individual case studies.[3]

The tests assisted in bringing the boy's unique themes of experience into focus without constraining him to respond in predetermined ways. Instead, a boy's responses to them reflected the structure of his individual subjective world. They also allowed the researcher the opportunity to look at the unconscious and more guarded aspects of the youth's personality. Such techniques encouraged the subjects to provide richly elaborated responses with a minimum of reflective awareness.

The case studies found in Chapters 2, 3, and 4 were based on the many hours of in-depth clinical interviews with Jerome, Pete, and Sly and the interpretations of their responses to the projective tests. Like any client who is engaged in a therapeutic relationship, each of these adolescents employed a number of self-defending psychological mechanisms in order to avoid looking at his own self-destructive behavior and deny the researcher access to his inner life. It was evident, however, that each young man's wish to be understood gradually overcame the reluctance to make painful self-disclosures. Although they were free to put a halt to the interview, none of them ever made the decision to end the unique alliance that was built between the interviewer and himself. The case studies in the following chapters demonstrate how Jerome, Pete, and Sly underwent the rigors of self-discovery, thereby putting each boy's delinquent behavior in a clinical and personal perspective for the first time.

---

[3]The Thematic Apperception Test and the Sentence Completion Test were respectively interpreted using guidelines established by Bellak (1975) and Holsapple and Miale (1954).

2

The Case
of Jerome

It is in the context of a youngster's psychological struggle from infancy to adolescence that his long history of delinquency must be looked at. In the case of Jerome, his delinquent behavior cannot be isolated from the disturbances in his psychological development. The question to be explored is how his antisocial acts are related to his psychological world. What is the meaning of the delinquency in Jerome's life? Furthermore, how is his particular kind of delinquency related to the disturbances in his psychological development? Is it possible to understand why his delinquent behavior took one form and not another?

JEROME: HIS SELF-PRESENTATION

Although 18 years old, Jerome could easily be taken for someone a few years older. About 5 feet, 10 inches tall, he was a stockily built, dark-skinned Afro-American male who gave off an air of being well dressed even though he was wearing the same khaki uniform issued to all the inmates at the Glenville State Training School. His clothing was so sharply creased that it looked as if it had been starched, pressed, and put on only minutes earlier. His hair was cut short and styled in the waves that were currently popular with black boys and required a great deal of brushing to achieve the desired effect. Although he smoked cigarettes throughout the first interview, his teeth were noticeably white and free of nicotine stains. Unlike many of his fellow inmates, Jerome had no hint of body odor. In fact, his neatness and cleanliness made him stand out as different from the other boys whose personal grooming standards rarely remained intact to the degree that Jerome's had.

Jerome's Personal History

Talking about himself and his family, Jerome said it had been his mother who always supported the four children in the family by working at various jobs, most recently as a nurse (the records indicated that she was a nurse's aide). Each one of the four children had different fathers—he himself was the youngest child. When he was quite young—he was not sure exactly how old he was at the time—his natural father and his father's girl friend took care of him at their place. His recollection was that he went to live with his father and this woman because his mother "wouldn't treat me right. Most of the time I wasn't staying with her." But the time spent in his father's home ended abruptly:

> My father's girl friend was beating me when I was small. And he put me on the doorstep and ran. And this, that's when, you know, my mother took the towels, I mean, the cloths off me, and started looking at scars and stuff, you know. And like, she said, like, you know, I was messed up and everything, you know.

He had not seen his father since that day he had been placed on the doorstep and taken back in by his mother. Even as a very young child, he found it hard to get along with his mother: "But, like, when I listening to her I really hated it, you know, to hear it, you know." Recalling how he handled his mother's orders to go to school, he said:

> When I was small, you know, .I ain't never go to school or nothing. I just said, "Fuck it, I ain't going to school." And it seemed like it was all right to school you, but it wasn't there for me, you know . . . My mother always, like, you know, let me, tell me to go to school, you know. Well, when I was younger, you know, I'd go to school, but as I was starting to grow up, school, you know, didn't really, wasn't for me, you know. I said, "Fuck it," you know, "I'll hang out with the boys."

Although it was cloudy in his mind, Jerome thought he had begun stealing things when he was 9 years old. His first theft took place during the 1967 riots in the city of Newark, where he was born and raised. He recalled that he did it in the presence of an aunt who encouraged him to "take stuff" from a liquor store. (Jerome may have been inaccurate in associating his first delinquent act with the Newark riots, because he would have been only 5 or 6 years old in 1967, not 9 as he had remembered it. On the other hand, he might have been wrong about how old he was when he started stealing things.) He put it this way:

> when I was small I used to be around, like I went to the riot that was in Newark . . . Like, I was small then, you know. My aunt, she, you know, broke into a liquor store. It was really broke in, but it was open and there was nobody in there. So, you know, we stole all the stuff and brung it to the house. Them National Guards beat me, and I started stealing from there. Then I started growing up.

Then I started following my brother. I've done robbery, uhm, snatching, you know, purse snatching and uhm, that was my main thing, you know.

When he was younger, his mother would beat him if he did not go to school or after he had been caught stealing. But he also remembered her beating him for nothing, and said he still had marks on his body from the whippings. After getting a beating he would "be feeling quite down and I would see if I could find me some money." Finding some money, it turned out, was stealing it from his mother or snatching some other woman's purse. With the money he stole he would buy a bag of marijuana, go to a movie, and "cool out." As he grew older he would run away from his mother to avoid a beating, and his mother finally gave up trying to use corporal punishment to make him obey her. At this point he felt he had begun to gain the upper hand in their relationship by outrunning her, telling her lies and half-truths, and continuing to steal. He would laugh at her and not listen to her verbal reprimands—the only weapon she had left. "I would let all her shit go in one ear and out the other." He would say to himself, "I got over and played with her mind and shit."

As soon as Jerome talked about the "fucked up" relationship with his mother, he added quickly that when looking back, he felt that she had been fair, and it was his fault that he did not listen to her:

Well, she had to do a lot for me 'cause she, she, ahah, birth me. And she birth me to come into this world. And it really was her fault 'cause of sex. And sometimes that I feel as though it is my fault in a sense, too, but it is both of ours, you know. I didn't listen.

He also did not express his anger verbally to her; he never cursed her. All he could do when he was near her was look at her harshly or look away.

During these early years, Jerome's mother had a series of men living with her and had a serious drinking habit for which she had been hospitalized twice. Jerome complained that "all my mother care about are drinking, her men, and sex." About the man living with her at present, Jerome made it very clear that the man was not his own father, but just his mother's current boyfriend:

She had several boyfriends. She had several before, each before she had him. But, you know, I have to realize that when she told me, you know, she had her own life to live, I said, "quite naturally she gonna get what she wanna get anyway," you know. She always telling people (angrily), "I am 50 something years old and I have four kids and like they always doing wrong," you know.

Jerome's account of his recent years was somewhat muddled in its chronology, which was not surprising in view of the number of programs he had entered and left. Since age 16 he had been a ward of the state and had served two stints in the training school at Glenville. Before going to Glenville the first time, he had been sent to the Essex County Workhouse for 5 months for armed robbery — the weapon he had carried was a butcher knife. Shortly afterwards, he was put in a halfway house run by the Vindicate Society. About his experience there, he said:

> It was a program, you know, ah, help you build, you know, yourself up. Get you ready for when you go outside, right. So, I didn't really function there right. But, you know, I got kicked out of there. I was there for like 9 months, right.

But he got into even more serious trouble at the Vindicate Society program when he broke into the office and stole money that belonged to his fellow detainees. He took the money, he explained, to get even with the staff for accusing him falsely of the crime of gun possession.

Following Jerome's release from the Vindicate Society program, the state placed him in a foster home, but he did not last long there. When his foster mother discovered that he was stealing from her purse, she threw him out of the house and he was once again without a roof over his head. His own mother would not have him back in her house, but eventually his older sister offered to take him in to stay with her family. He was subsequently convicted of stealing from her and was sent back to the Glenville State Training School for a second time. After serving 4 months of a 6-month term he was paroled.

It was toward the end of Jerome's second term at the training school that the interviews with him began. His imminent parole was very much on his mind. Just prior to his discharge he talked about how he intended to try to make it on his own and not be dependent on his mother. It was important for him to be independent, he said, because his mother had informed him when he was 16 that she "had a life to live on her own and I had a life to live. So we have to live apart." He went on to explain it this way:

> So, I know that what she was saying in her own type of way, you know. But, I really didn't understand it. I'm no baby no longer — I'm suppose to be a grown man, 18 years old. I have to make some type of stand for myself. I have made a lot of mistakes in my life and I still are making mistakes, you know. I know ain't nobody out here for you, you know. Because you make lots of mistakes, you know. I know the mistakes I made, I realize it, but I just don't care at times when I do it.

He felt certain he could make it on his own this second time after he was paroled. What he hoped to do was to make a home for his girl friend who was 17 years old, and their baby.

> J: Did you know I have a baby?
> I: No I didn't.

J: Yeah, a boy. He's 3 months old. I ain't seen him yet, you know, but I'm, you know, proud about that.

I: What are you proud about?

J: That, that, you know, like, to be a father. It, you know, make me feel good, you know, that I made a baby, you know.

I: It makes you feel like a man because you made a baby?

J: Well, like, you know, yeah. I feel like, I, you know, I really done something. Yeah, you know, yeah, he's 3 months old. Yeah, I done something, you know.

I: What are your plans for the baby and its mother when you get out of here (the penal facility)?

J: I, like, well, I want to take care of them, you know. I want to get a place, you know, where we can live. I heard, you know, that he look like, you know, he look like me.

I: I guess you were happy to hear that he looks like you.

J: Yeah, you know, yeah. I, you know, I was happy.

However, instead of acting on this idea of getting a place for the three of them to live, he went to his mother and asked her if he could live with her. When she told him once again that she did not have room for him, he was very angry, he said, with her and her boyfriend. "I didn't have no place to go so I went to Proof," the halfway house for juveniles leaving prison. "Well, it was, it was just a place where you can go, ahm, you can go there and stay, work, stay there for like 6 month, work, you know. That was it, but I left."

The period following this parole and the time at Proof House was a time of drifting, aimlessness, and general confusion. He had no home. Several people gave him a place to live and board when he was destitute—he expressed his gratitude and appreciation for their good will by robbing them. He took a camera from the home of a man who had given him temporary lodging until he was able to make other arrangements. He stole a radio from a family who gave him housing and meals and had held his clothing for him as he drifted from place to place. In both cases the thefts were reported to the police. The only bright spot during this dark and gloomy period was his happening on a job skills program at a local chapter of the Urban League. At this place he found a black female counselor to whom he became very much attached. Describing her as being more of a mother to him than his natural mother, he said:

I'll go to the store for Mrs. Thomas (the counselor) first before I'd go to the store for my mother. 'Cause like Mrs. Thomas gives me some money to go to the store and she tell me to get this, that, or the other. I get it for her. And I just had met her; I've been in this here program for like aah, aah, 10 weeks, 11 weeks. Eleven or 12 weeks. I'll go to the store for her before I'll go for anybody, you know. And like if my mother send me to the store I'll go and don't come back. Then she really be pissed off. She be saying, "Well, Jerome, why you do this, why you do that?" you know. I say, I don't say nothing. I look at her.

Continuing the contrast between the counselor and his mother, Jerome stated:

> My mother has four kids and every time she gets a problem, she say, "Well, Jerome, if you get in trouble, somebody will call my house and say, "Mrs. Emory, your son got in trouble." Then she'll say "Well, I got four kids and I've tried my best!" Either you're going to help me, I your son, either you're going to help me or what, you know. I'm saying, "What is it, you're going to help me or what?" I can come to Mrs. Thomas and say, "Mrs. Thomas, you know, I'm in a little trouble," you know. She'll say, "We'll see if we can help you." I try to understand to a certain extent how my mother really is, but I can't. Like she say she got her life to live and I got my life to live. I would imagine that I know that already 'cause I'm out here in the world trying to make it the best that I can. I can't say if, and, or but about it. I'm out here, you know, and ain't nobody helping me. Yeah, she is helping me, right. She is helping me, money, like I need two dollars she'll give it to me. She'll give it to me. She gave me money to stay at a hotel because I didn't have no place to stay, you know. My mother wouldn't do that, she'd say, "I don't have any money," you know.

Mrs. Thomas' loyalty and unswerving support were tested numerous times by Jerome and not found wanting. When he was arrested for various kinds of larcenies he always called on her to get him out of his difficulties. Thus far, she had always come to his rescue. When Jerome completed the job skills training Mrs. Thomas even went so far as to back him for enrollment in a federally funded job training program at another location over the objections of her fellow staff members who were acquainted with Jerome's past record and were of the opinion that he would reflect badly on the Urban League. They proved to be correct in their estimate of him. Jerome was suspended from the program for 30 days for not complying with the rules limiting smoking to some designated areas, but he was allowed to return to the facility after he approached the director for reconsideration. At the time of the last interview, he was still enrolled in this program.

JEROME'S INNER WORLD

The study of Jerome's psychological world was conducted on two levels simultaneously. At one level there were in-depth interviews carried on with him in the prison facility, at the various training programs and at different places in the city of Newark. At a second and deeper level Jerome was asked to respond to a selected series of photographs from the Thematic Apperception Test and to the items in the Sentence Completion Test. What follows is an attempt to analyze these materials by putting together how Jerome portrayed himself directly in the interviews with what can be inferred about him on the basis of his projective productions. The aim was to understand how his delinquent acts may have been related to his psychological development.

Relationships with Women

Strangely enough—or possibly it should be phrased as logically enough, many of Jerome's projective images were not so different from what he talked about freely in the interviews, for he openly and unblushingly spoke of his love for and his anger with his mother without much disguise or embarrassment. It was as though he was a young child, sometimes even a baby, crying for his mother's affection and having a tantrum when she failed to pick him up and hug and kiss him. At age 18 he had not released her from his childish demands for immediate gratification, while at the same time he was struggling to free himself of this person who made him so dependent on her and angry enough to want to "take and choke her."

AMBIVALENT BOND TO MOTHER

If I had the opportunity I would stay with my mother the rest of my life. But I'm at the time of my life; I have to get out on my own . . . I still want to be with her.

This was Jerome's cry that he uttered just prior to being paroled from the Glenville Training School for the second time. Pushed out into the world by his mother before he was ready or able to make it on his own, Jerome at age 18 still wanted to be close to her again, even though he knew she would refuse to allow him to return home. He realized it was time for him to make a life of his own without her. The ambivalence he felt to a mother he longed for so deeply and at the same time needed to free himself from almost as desperately appeared in his response to TAT card 4:

They look madly in love. Look like he's trying to pull away from her when she's trying to get his attention. But he look very, very angry at her, but she trying very much to get his attention. He seems as though he don't want her attention, I mean, to have her attention. So he looking at something else. (So, what happens in the end?) . . . I can't, she kisses. (Anything else?) That's it.

Although the couple was seen by him as being "madly in love," the woman was at the same time violating the hero's psychological and personal space. Angry about the female's attempts to become the center of his attention, the hero did not like the woman's effort to become his focal point and attempted to reject her demands. In a way similar to what Jerome stated during his interviews, the thematic material in response to the TAT stimulus revealed his perception that he and his mother loved each other but that he had to break away from her influence over him.

To TAT card 13B, which depicts a small boy sitting in the doorway of a dilapidated house, Jerome responded with confused ambivalence over how to handle the push and pull of the conflicting and imperious needs to be taken care of and at the same time to harm the caretaker who had failed to provide for him:

> He look hungry, aah . . . he look . . . hungry. Wants somebody to care for him. He don't like the way he's living. Ah, he gets up and walk away. He gets a rock and comes back and sit down. Has his hand up on his chin. (What happens in the end?) He walks back and sit down.

The child's hunger was seen by Jerome as being not merely for food, but for "somebody to care for him." What should the hero do to satisfy his hunger? The hero's behavior mirrored Jerome's ambivalence. First he left the scene and picked up a rock presumably to hurl at the source of his hunger. Then he came back and sat down but did not throw it. He just continued sitting down holding the rock in one hand and his chin in the other, unable to act. His ambivalence had immobilized him. The problem of not liking the way he was living was unresolved by the hero just as it was in Jerome's life.

Jerome finished item 1 of the Sentence Completion Test by putting into words the way he wished he had been treated when he was younger. He phrased this in terms of a child's right to be cared for: "Children are usually certain that *they should be children.*" In other words, children should be allowed to act like children rather than having to be adults before they have matured enough to assume adult responsibilities. Jerome was defending his right to feel dependent on his mother, a subject he said in his interviews she constantly harped on, reminding him that he was old enough to take care of himself. His sense of not being capable of being independent of her was mentioned in the interviews and also expressed in the sentence completion items 4 and 6. To item 4 he replied, "A person is most helpless when *they are by themself, when they are trying to build themself up.*" He completed item 6 with these words: "The hardest decision is *when you are going out on your own.*"

When Jerome had problems and felt helpless to solve them himself, he would run back to his mother with the expectation that she would bail him out. On one occasion he tried to persuade her to help him get his job back at the same place she was employed and where he had worked too until he had quit. He explained how angry he felt when she refused to help him.

> I wanted to get the job right then. And, my mother, right, my mother told me, I said, "Ma," she helped me get the job there the first time anyway, right. So, my mother said, uhm, she said, aah, I said (softly), "Ma, could you help me get back in there again?" She know I left it before to come here (federally funded program).

She said, "I'm not gonna help you. You help yourself. How do you think it would make me feel you to coming back?" So, I just didn't bug her.

On the basis of this version of the incident it appeared as if he had accepted his mother's explanation for not helping him again. But when asked more about it, he said he felt that it was his mother's "obligation" to help him again. When she failed to accept this responsibility—which he saw as being hers—he became very angry with her. "Fuck it," he said to himself and hung up on his mother by "slamming" down the receiver. "I was fired up because she wouldn't talk to me." Actually his mother had talked with him, but the content of her conversation, rejecting his request, was what he found intolerably frustrating. Jerome seemed to think that things must go his way immediately, just as soon as he wanted them to take place, and especially where his mother was involved. Because he had put himself on the line to some degree by asking her to do something for him, he had made himself dependent on her and vulnerable to being rejected by her. Yet he kept making appeals for her help even though he knew she would hurt him by failing to respond in the way he wished.

Jerome had been out on his own since he was 16 trying, as he put it, to build himself up when he neither wanted to nor was prepared to leave his mother for full-fledged entry into the outside world. His deep ambivalence about staying and leaving were expressed in his story to TAT card 6BM.

Look like he's leaving his mother. She very upset. He's thing 'bout he, he very worried about leaving and he, he know he has to leave 'cause he have a life to live on his own. He don't want, too old to stay with his mother. So, his mother say, "Oh, my, you're leaving. I don't want you to leave." And he just depressed, looking down.

The hero of the story looks as though he's about to leave his mother but holds back because he's very worried about taking the step. Jerome has put into the hero's mind the very argument his mother had made to him and that he has repeated so often in the interviews—that he was too old and therefore he could not stay with his mother because they both had to live their own lives. But in his response to TAT card 6BM, Jerome's strong wish to remain with her was projected on his mother. He fantasized that she was pleading with him to stay with her, and he put those wonderful words in her mouth—the ones that she had never spoken in real life—"Oh, my, you're leaving. I don't want you to leave." And she was also "very upset" at the thought that he might leave.

But the pleasure at hearing those fond entreaties and seeing her upset at the possibility that he might leave did not succeed in settling his worries. Just as he had walked back and sat down in his story about the hungry child, here also the conclusion was that the hero was "just depressed, looking down." His ambivalence over the attachment and separation from his mother prevented him from taking real solace from her invitation not to leave. He knew he was no longer a child and he had to make the break. Describing the hero as being depressed demonstrated his sense of loss of the mothering he felt he never had and his self-doubt over his own capacity to fend for himself. Both of the stories ended with the hero unable to bring the plot to a resolution: "He walks back and sit down" and "And he just depressed, looking down."

When Jerome talked about the hurts he had experienced in his encounters with his mother, the most crucial and crushing instances had been those times when he felt she had treated him as though he were insignificant and unwanted.

> My mother treat me as though you are just there. Come to ask for money, you eat . . . whatever, you just there. She care about her man, having sex or you know, whatever they have, drink or whatever, you know. She cares more about that than she care about us.

He felt ignored and pushed out of her life by her appetites for drink and sex with her young lovers. In item 62 of the Sentence Completion Test he projected his wish on her that "She couldn't bear to touch *a man.* " Because we know that his mother has touched many men and not been close to him, it would be his wish that his mother could not bear to touch or give so much attention to those other males who were in her bed but would instead shower all of her attention and love onto him—to want him and to touch him. His sexual fantasies about his mother and his enormous wish to be close to her and wanted by her were expressed openly when he said:

> If she cared more about us she wouldn't ever have that motherfucking man in the house. She would have me sleeping in the bed with her. But we wouldn't be having physical sex, but we, I would be just sleeping in the bed even though she got one room, you know.

Possibly he wanted to sleep at her side and be tended to and touched in a fashion he sensed he had never been as an infant and young child.

> If I had the opportunity I would stay with my mother the rest of my life. But I'm at the time of my life I know I have to get out on my . . . I still wanted to be with her . . . I would like for her, me and her to be more together."

Jerome has had a long history of petty thievery. From an early age he began taking money from his mother's purse even though he knew, as he put it, it "wasn't cool for me to do."

> I used to take things . . . from her, too, you know, which wasn't cool for me to do . . . That was about it, money, you know. I didn't want to ask for it, I knew I could just take it. Come back at any time I wanted to come back in . . . If I asked

her for it she probably would give it to me or either she would tell me to work for it. I don't like waiting for things, you know.

Although stealing from his mother can be interpreted in one sense as a way of behaving aggressively towards her out of anger and resentment over being mistreated and pushed out of her life, at the same time such acts can also be viewed as attempts to secure a part (a possession) of his mother for himself. As he said, he could "come back at any time I wanted to come back in." Stealing from her was his means of getting some of his mother's love. He wanted to take from her what she did not give to him—money, car, attention, affection, sexual love, all of which she gave so freely to her adult male lovers who lived with her.

When responding to TAT card 5, which is a picture of a woman looking into a room, Jerome told this story: "She opened the door because she thought she hear a burglar. And, she do see someone. He push her down the steps." The burglar committed two aggressive acts against the older woman—theft and physical aggression. The first, the act of stealing, may have been Jerome's way of once again stating his wish to be in possession of a part of his mother's life by taking something from her. The second, an act of physical aggression, may be an expression of his anger. The mode chosen was an act of rejection to cover his overriding sense of dependency. By pushing her down the steps, he symbolically freed himself of her. He was angry and openly aggressive toward the person who had *pushed* him out of her life and into the world—his mother, so he stole from her and then got rid of her by pushing her down the stairs. As in his real life the burglar not only got into trouble by stealing but by the problems involved in dealing with his pent-up rage, which resulted from his mother's denying him what he wanted.

Other adult women also became targets of his unbroken series of attempts to secure by theft what he wanted and had not received from his mother. At 16 when his mother had put him out of her place, his older sister offered to provide him with a place to live. He responded to his sister's generous effort to help him by stealing money from her—from the very person who had come to his rescue during his time of need. His explanation for this behavior was simply that he needed the money and had asked his sister to give him $20.00 to go into New York City to see a movie and get a supply of marijuana. When she refused he stole the money from her welfare payment, which he knew was for paying the rent and purchasing the food for him, his sister, and her six children. Because she did not give him what he had requested he grew angry and felt justified in taking what he wanted. In fact, he stated that he felt rejected, hurt, and small when being told "no." This act of thievery served as a means of hurting his sister to the degree that he had been harmed in being denied and rejected.

Jerome appeared to treat each individual incident as though it occurred in a vacuum without precedent or ongoing history. It meant very little to him that his sister was the same person who provided him with food and shelter when there was no other person coming to his aid. It only mattered to him that his immediate request was not satisfied.

This pattern of stealing from females who attempted to assist him was deeply entrenched—he behaved the same way toward a foster mother in whose home he was placed after he was expelled from the halfway house for stealing and was without any place to live. Even knowing his history the woman was willing to take a chance with him. Jerome said he had hoped she would be the person who would help to turn him around, but it did not work out that way.

> I was getting into so much trouble they placed me with, with a foster mother. And, like, uhm, I really wasn't listening to what she was saying. I started stealing from her and doing what I wanted to do and was coming in any, and coming in, whatever time I wanted to come in, you know.

In both of these instances of his sister and foster mother, he took from them what he felt he could not get in any other way. Each of these women had other men in their lives whom they also had to attend and respond to—like his mother who had men in her life. In the case of his sister she had a husband as well as six children who also required her emotional and monetary resources. The problem with his foster mother was connected with the privileges she granted her natural son.

> There I think I was really going behind her son 'cause her son was like, uhm, he was like, he had his mother's car and he got down on the car, you know. Like, when he knew his mother was at work he came back to the house, you know. Wanted me, help, you know, snatch pocketbooks here, you know. He want to get enough gas, you know, or whatever.

In this account Jerome tried to give the impression that he had been made to snatch his foster mother's purse. But this was a major, longstanding feature of his repertoire. The more important reason that he stole from this woman appeared to be that she gave her son access to her car. She, like his mother, was giving another man who was a rival for her attention a token of love and autonomy, a car, that was denied him. Jerome has previously stated that he was angry with his mother because he suspected she had bought her live-in lover a Seville Cadillac. When a replay of what happened at home began to take place at the foster home, Jerome could not bear reliving the old situation. Instead of being angry with the male involved he took out his hurt and aggression on the woman as he had done to his mother. By stealing from his foster mother he was getting a part of her he felt she had denied him. His enormous feelings of deprivation and envy overrode his sense of gratitude and appreciation for the warm and secure physical aspects of his foster home.

Jerome wanted what his male rival had attained—a car. Although a car for him was seen as being a gift from a woman, it was also a means of transportation to escape or leave behind the person who provided the gift. A car symbolized autonomy and distance from his mother and other women. The importance of an automobile for Jerome was seen in two of his sentence completion responses. To item 72 he said, "If one cannot own *a car.*" Although the idea was incomplete, it did indicate that a car was important to him. Jerome might have been saying that because he could not own a car, he did not see himself as a significant and meaningful person. From his perspective, you were only worthwhile if a woman gave you a car. His doubts and ambivalence concerning his ability to master a car—a symbol of autonomy—was seen in sentence completion item 69. He said, "When the car skidded *it hit someone.*" Even if he had a car, he would not know how to handle it properly and be in control of it. He would wind up harming someone, maybe himself.

BAD MOTHER–GOOD MOTHER

Jerome repeatedly stated that he experienced his mother as being less than a mother should be to her child. His idea of a mother was someone who should be there at all times to bail him out of his various scrapes and difficulties. About asking for things from his mother, he said:

> She'll start crying or do whatever and I just don't want to see her cry. And when I ask her for such a thing, "Nah, I don't have it," you know. Then I get "I know you have it (angrily)." Then I be wanting to take it from her, you know. But with Mrs. Thomas, "Do you have a dollar or two dollars?" "Here Jerome," like that, she don't give me no lecture, "Go do this with it, go do that."

Although his mother had, from his perspective, been inadequate he had found a good mother in the likes of a black middle-aged female counselor at the Urban League job skills program he attended.

> And like, I really care for that lady, you know. But I care for her in my own way. I don't care for her as though I want to make love with her or, you know, I want to marry her. I feel as though I like her in a way as though I want her to be my mother. But I know she ain't my mother really, but she treat me just like a mother. A real mother, too. And, like she'll try to explain things which, you know, she, she, she like to have fun, you know. And when it's time to be serious, she be serious, you know. 'Cause like, this suppose to be a business place (referring to the Urban League office). All right, when I, you know, when I feel like playing, I play with her, whatever, and she play with me too, whatever. And like, whatever she ask me to do I'll do it. 'Cause I feel as though, "yeah, Mrs. Thomas, whatever you ask me to do I'll do it 'cause I feel you did a lot for me." She did do a lot for me. At the

period of time I been here she did a lot for me, you know. And I bless her for that, yep.

Jerome saw in this woman the "real mother" or the good mother that he had been clamoring for all of his life, one who was able and willing to listen and to provide for him. He maintained that he loved her and would never do anything to hurt her and if he did he said, "I would be hurting myself. She just like a little part of me. She really do help me." Continuing to define how he felt about his integral connection with the two women, Jerome said: "'Cause, see, my mother, you know, I still, you know, I suppose to be a part of her." Jerome's need to be "part" of his mother and to experience Mrs. Thomas as "a little part of me" both reflected his arrested psychological development. He had yet to individuate and separate from the dominant mother figures in his life. Even with seeing his natural mother as not being "a real mother" in contrast to Mrs. Thomas, he still wanted to sleep with her. He had been unable to fully separate from his mother figures, seeing himself as being unable to go it alone. To function he felt that he must be in continual physical and psychological contact with his mother. Moreover, his sense of identity was very much tied up with his mother's, who represented a significant part of himself, functioning as "selfobjects" in the sense described by Kohut (1971, 1977). Without having this incorporation of his mothers he was afraid that he was nothing and that he would even cease to exist. Such symbiotic closeness—usually observed in infants who are a few months old—was desired by Jerome who was chronologically a young adult.

Jerome's arrested psychological development further highlighted the series of traumas he suffered as an infant when he did not have a stable mother–infant relationship. Being abandoned and abused by his mother and his father's girl friend he had not known the closeness of a warm, secure mother–infant relationship. It appeared that his natural mother was so preoccupied with her own life that she wanted Jerome to grow up and be away from her, even when he was small, young, and highly dependent. The shattering resulting from these early disruptions made it impossible for him to separate from his mother and become a psychologically independent person.

In expressing his need to keep these mother figures as a "part" of him, Jerome gave evidence that he "knows" there had been problems in his mother's relationship to him. Even though he could not remember what had happened in those early years of his life, he "knows" that he was mistreated by her even as a baby and very young child and also that he had never possessed the security of a close relationship with her. That symbiotic attachment with Jerome, which his mother either terminated prematurely or never formed at all, was still being sought by him in his need to be part of his mother and adult women and for them to be part of him.

Jerome looked to his newly formed mother-substitute, the middle-aged Mrs. Thomas, to provide him with the steady stream of support he believed his mother had denied him all his life. He tested her intentions and the boundaries of her generosity as a young child would. Actually, to hear Jerome talk about being a part of her and her being a "real mother" sounded as though he was describing the relationship between a mother and an infant, not between an adult and a young man. Side by side with this level of relating to her, however, Jerome had other feelings about her. When he discussed how he felt about her, he made two disclaimers about how he thought about behaving towards her.

> Most people hurt other people, but I can't do that, you know. I mean, I can do it, you know, I know I'm capable of doing it, *but I don't think,* I wouldn't do it to her. I feel as though she's been more of a mother to me than my mother really been to me. And, like, I really care for that lady, you know. But I care for her in my own way. *I don't care for her as though I want to make love with her* or, you know, I want to marry her. I feel as though I like her in a way though I want her to be my mother.

In making these disclaimers he stated that he would not react toward the female counselor, Mrs. Thomas, in two specific ways: He would not steal from her nor would he make sexual advances toward her, because she was like a mother to him. Because in actuality he had taken advantage of many women it seemed as though he was saying that he had to watch himself with this particular woman because such behavior was almost automatic for him. This pattern of hurting the women who attempted to help him was of long duration and a major facet of his interaction with them. He knew that he was not only "capable of doing it," but that he had done it most of his life. Realizing that the pattern was so much a part of his personality he could not be fully certain whether he would steal from her or make sexual advances toward her or not: "I know I'm capable of doing it, but I don't think, I wouldn't do it to her." One aspect of what the "it" referred to was his previous acts of thievery from women—thefts from the purses of his mother and other females.

The second disclaimer was that he did not wish to have sex with or marry Mrs. Thomas. For Jerome, sexual appetites were very much associated with his mother. He regarded her as a woman who is very much enmeshed and tied to her physical appetites—sex and alcohol. He felt he had been rejected and discarded by her because she was so involved with her own physical pleasures. The other men in her life, her lovers, shared her bed—the place where she gave her love to them, not to him. Although it might be unspeakable for him to say that he wanted to make love and marry his counselor, whom he regarded as a mother figure, this was the type of closeness he had craved from his mother. Being denied this maternal closeness, he was always seeking it in his relationships with older women. So the disclaimer served to tell him that he should not allow himself to have such feelings toward the counselor—the real and good mother—even though he might want to be in her bed in the same way the other men were in his mother's bed. This might have been his way of indicating to himself that such behavior towards his good mother was taboo. Nevertheless he still hungered for this type of physical and emotional closeness to his mother and mother substitute.

OLDER WOMEN–YOUNGER WOMEN

Although he felt that he had been able to control his sexual feelings toward Mrs. Thomas, the counselor, there had been other women in helping and nurturing roles toward whom he had made sexual advances or had thought of doing so, although most frequently he had failed to make the moves he had in mind:

> J: See, oh, I uhm, I used to talk to this psychologist at Mt. Carmel Guild (a social service agency). I used to talk to her, was about to pop the question to her. Every time I came there she say, "Tell me what is ever on your mind." She said, "What do you have to hold back your shit for, man? Tell me whatever it is. I'll wait." I don't know why I ain't never tell her neither. I ain't never tell her. She, you know, I got quiet and she always make me draw pictures and stuff, you know. I was always quiet, always wanted, always would stare. She would say, "J, why are you staring at me like that?" I'd say, "Just looking, that's all." I never told her, you know, but always wanted to, you know. Like after I leave her office, I'd say "Damn, I should have told her."

He also had sexual feelings toward his teacher.

> I tried to get my teacher. She works at East Orange General Hospital. She works at Crisis, that's like you got a problem you call in and they write it down. And I call her and she, we be talking and everything, you know. She ask if you're having a good time, if you're in school or where you live. She was all right . . . I used to sit right here and like, there was a big table and I used to put my hand under there and feel her legs. She used to say, "Stop, J!" I'd say, "Come on, Gail," you know, and she'd say, "Bug out," you know. 'Cause I had to see a psychologist and a doctor there 'cause I don't know, I had a temper.

Although Jerome attempted to present himself to me and others as a ladies' man, he did not always bring his sexual advances to a successful conclusion and sometimes he failed to make any overt approach even though he fantasized about sex with the women who were helping him. The woman whose leg he touched dismissed him by telling him to "bug out." With the psychologist who had emplored him to say what was on his mind, his mind was filled with sexual fantasy, but he was always reluctant to expose his desires to her. He may have been afraid of being rejected, because he had some doubts about being a competent lover with these more sophisticated women. Even with his fears, the desire to be close to older women was very much present.

Jerome's explanation for his preference for older women and his relationship to them was discussed by the two of us.

J: Mrs. Whatamacallit say I have some type of whatamacallit, man, you know, she said, "You always get the ladies, the older ladies."

I: Is that something you do consciously?

J: I don't know, but that is what she said, yeah is that what she said. But I don't know.

I: Is that something you try to do, you feel you go after these older ladies?

J: Not really (laughs). Not really unless I want them to. Seriously, not unless I want them to.

I: But you do want them to, I guess.

J: Yeah (proudly), you know, (changing the focus) like, I like older people, you know.

I: What do you get from older women you cannot get from younger girls?

J: A lot. I know this here one girl, I didn't tell you about her, I even forgot her name. I was at the bus stop catching the 25 Bus. She asked me if my name was such and such. I said, "No." She said, "You look like a certain person I know." . . . She said, "You want to play some paddle ball?" just like that, you know. She ain't ask me my name. We still playing paddle ball, she said, "What's your name?" "My name Jerome," and she tells me hers, but I forgot it. Then, aah, after we played she said if I wanted to go to a bar and have a drink. I said I didn't want any, and she said, "Why, you don't have any money?" I said, "No, that's not it, I just don't want one." She said, "Come on, I'll buy you one." Then we started walking and walking and she bought one, you know. And we started kissing and everything. Then we started seeing more of each other, particularly, you know. That's when I was at Essex County College (the location of a job skills program conducted by the Urban League). She came down there all the time sitting out there waiting for me and everything. I said, "Haay," you know, then we go and do it.

I: What happened to her?

J: I just didn't want to see her no more.

I: Why was that?

J: I just got tired of her.

I: What made you get tired of her?

J: Huh?

I: What happened you got tired of her? Something must have happened that you got tired of her. Something must have happened that you got tired of.

J: She just wasn't my thing, I guess.

I: She wasn't your thing or she wanted your thing?

J: She just wanted my thing (his penis).

I: Had you been sleeping with her?

J: Yeah.

I: How old was she?

J: She was aah, in her thirties. She was like, she wanted me to go to her husband's house and beat him up. She said, "I want you to go over his house and beat him up." I said, "Yeah, I can go over there and kick his you know," and we both laughed. I told her, "Yeah, I'm down (willing to do it)." She said, "I'm going to move with my mother anyway," which she did. She started moving with her mother the next day.

I: Were you living with her or what?

J: No, I didn't live with her; she used to take me to cheap hotels (braggingly).

I: How did you feel about that?

J: It was all right, uhm, she used to always get a radio from the man downstairs when you pay your money. She'd say, "I'll leave a $5.00 deposit 'til you get your radio back. I'll give it back in the morning.' He'd say, "Okay, no problem as long as you bring it back."

I: So you're the lover.

J: Yeah, you know.

In his encounters with women Jerome wanted to be seen by them as being in control, being the competent aloof male. But behind this mask of macho maleness was a penniless and destitute young boy. The older woman in the case described had provided the resources to help keep the sexually based relationship afloat. Although Jerome gave the impression that he was proud of his ability to attract a 30-year-old woman, the most exciting aspect of the affair for him was not so much in the sex they had as the fact that she asked him to beat up her husband. This permitted him to feel good because he was not only sleeping with the man's wife and getting the psychic satisfaction of beating out a male rival in the sexual sphere, but he was also enjoying the fantasy of beating up on this man physically. The idea of being successful in competition with an older male rival appeared to give him more satisfaction than the sex itself. Whereas previously he had been placed in the role of the inferior in his relationship to his mother's lovers, here he was the victor. He had won the prize in the form of the maternal figure and been asked to beat up her man to boot.

It has been suggested that Jerome preferred older women as a way of securing the maternal closeness he had been deprived of. Further support for this view could be seen in the discussion with him in which he contrasted younger with older females.

Well, aah, older ladies, you know, they can sit down and have a conversation, not being silly, not being uhm, uhm, they can be on a very serious basis . . . But I feel as though I can make it with them, you know, better than a younger person.

About older women he commented that they acted "more mature."

I think it's just the uhm, they act more comfortable. I just can't walk up to a younger person. They might say something smart. An older person tells you how they feel about something, you know, they don't beat around a bush or nothing. They're straightforward, you know, you know.

Although he stated older women "acted more comfortable," this might well have been a projection on his part—he was more comfortable with them. His comparison of older and younger women continued:

Say you walk up to a 17 or 18-year-old chick and, you know, you say, "I wanna talk to you, and stuff, baby." Who has time for doing a whole lot of stuff like that? And you could, could probably get her with your rap anyway, knowing that she's silly and you could play with her mind. But you don't want to do that, you know.

In saying that a younger woman had to be treated differently because she was immature and "silly," he appeared to see them as taking the very role and position he wanted to occupy with older women—the situation in which he was the one being nurtured and cared for. There would be too much required of him to be involved with a younger female who might have the same needs as he had. By calling them silly he seemed to perceive them as being helpless and weak, whereas he needed someone who would be strong enough to take care of him and themselves as well. There was room for only one baby in a relationship with Jerome. Possibly that was the reason he had not tried to carry out his plan to make a home for his young girl friend and their baby boy when he was paroled from the training school.

I: You had a baby by a girl before. What happened to that girl?
J: I don't see her no more.
I: What happened?
J: She moved and I don't see her no more.
I: Do you know where she is?
J: Nope. And I ain't tried looking for her either.
I: Why is that?
J: I ain't interested.
I: Something must have changed because at one time you were really into her.
J: Yeah, but I . . .
I: What changed? Something happened.
J: I just didn't, I just didn't bother looking for her. Wherever she is I figured she was real happy.
I: As I recall, the last time I saw you (just prior to his parole) the one thing we talked about was the baby, about what's her name?
J: JoAnne (the name of the mother of his child).
I: About JoAnne, okay about JoAnne and about how important they were to you. I'm surprised in a way that you have not looked for her.
J: Nah, she moved.
I: Yeah, I realize that, but even though you have not tried looking for her.
J: It is not important! They weren't really important (softly).

In fact, it might have been that his relationship with the woman in her 30's broke up because he was unable to be as mature as was expected of him. When he was initially asked why the relationship was terminated, he said, "I just got tired of her." On probing further about what occurred another story began to unfold.

J: You know something (stated in a rush), but I'm tired of that shit though (referring to his former middle-aged lover). She left me at the bus stop, but I got tired of that shit though! That's real, I just didn't want her around no more!

I: What did you get tired of?

J: Well, she, she wanted me to have oral sex with her. I wanted to, but, you know, I didn't think she was clean enough, you know. She ain't smell or anything, I just didn't want to do it. I didn't know her that good to have it, you know.

I: Would she have oral sex with you?

J: Ah, no, I told her, "No," she didn't do it to me, nothing like that. We stayed in, had all day and she kept bothering me. "You ready?" "Sh," I said, "you're bothering me like ten times." I said, "I'm asleep. Let me get some sleep." She didn't want me to get some sleep; she kept shaking me. Like, the radio is playing, she said, "Come on, Jerome, come on," you know (laughs).

I: How did you feel when she kept shaking you, she wanted some more?

J: (Blurting in) I was getting mad, I was getting angry, you know. 'Cause I said, "Come on, I'm sleepy, I wanna get some sleep.' I was tired.

I: What were you angry about?

J: Well, 'cause she kept pestering me, kept shaking me saying, "Come on, come on, come on," you know.

I: Were you a little embarrassed that she kept wanting it and you weren't ready?

J: Nah, I wasn't embarrassed. I was, I just didn't feel like it then. I was just tired.

I: That's what I'm saying, she kept wanting more and more and more and you weren't ready for it.

J: Uhuh, I was ready for it. You see, I had already done it to her twice, you know.

I: But she wanted more. You couldn't get it up?

J: Yeah; most definitely. Yeah, yep. I was ready, but I just said, "Nah, I don't feel like it. Nah."

I: But sometimes after a man has an orgasm he has to rest for a while while the woman is ready to keep going. She was ready to keep going, but you weren't ready. Right? Maybe it's hard for you to say that.

J: Right, true. (Defensively) I'm serious, but I was ready. I was ready, but you know, when I walked in the place I fell asleep. I don't know why. 'Cause everyday we were seeing each other she was telling me, "I'm horny, I'm horny." She wanted to take me to this place, that hotel, whatever.

I: So, sex was very important for her?

J: Yeah.

I: How did you feel about that?

J: And it still is for her, I bet she's finding every young man she can out there. Just like, when I see her downtown a couple a months ago . . . I said, "How you doing?" She said, "How you doing?" That was it. She walked out and started talking to somebody else.

Jerome found himself unable to perform to the degree sexually as requested by this mature woman—he was sexually and emotionally spent whereas she was eager to have more and more. He had climaxed twice and been left exhausted whereas she was raring to continue. Even when he described the two sexual sequences it sounds more like a fight—"I had already done it to her twice' '—than an experience of lovemaking. At the beginning he said he had refused to perform cunnilingus because she was not clean, but he then changed his reason to the fact he did not know her well enough. It seemed as though he had performed the best he could but it was insufficient. Apparently, it was the woman who had ended the relationship and discarded him, not the reverse, as he had claimed in a previous version of the affair. Although he talked about her derisively, saying, "I bet she's finding every young man she can out there," he knew she left him to find other young lovers to take his place. Being once again rejected by an older woman, it seemed as though he was left feeling impotent and incompetent.

During the relationship with this woman he wound up feeling woefully inadequate and impotent in much the same way he had felt with his mother. The termination of the relationship was also similar to what had happened between him and his mother. His mother and this woman each chose another man or men over him. Moreover, each chose men younger than themselves as a source of sexual pleasure and personal involvement. In the end they both discarded him.

The idea that he was attempting to fill the maternal void in his relationships with older women slipped out when we were talking about older women.

I: So, you prefer older women?

J: Yep.

I: So, maybe there are some things you can get from older women you can't get from young girls. Things like love, tenderness, support, clothes.

J: (Jumping in) Clothing.

I: Clothing, yeah. They give you all those kinds of things.

J: Right. (choked up) Plus, the ob, you see, my mother didn't give me that.

I: None of that.

J: No.

I: None at all?

J: Shh, she got no, she got no, you know, affection to make me feel as though I'm her, her son.

I: Sometimes she did and sometimes she didn't?

J: Yeah, 'cause like when she would beat me, right, I would say don't worry about that.

I: So, you would want to deny it?

J: I always denied it, every time she would beat me. Even though I went along or not. She'd curse and get fired up, threw shit, you know.

His sense of deprivation along with his desire for his mother were both encompassed in his complaint—"She got no, she got no, you know, affection to make me feel as though I'm her, her son." Yet when she had beaten him, cursed him, and threw things at him, he would say to her, "Don't worry about that." He could not bear to retaliate. Although he denied the expression of his enormous anger and hostility in her presence, he felt it very deeply and he was sometimes afraid it would get out of control. In the story he told in response to the stimulus of TAT card 13MF—a picture of a man in the foreground with his hand over his face and in the rear a woman partially clad lying on a bed—Jerome portrayed the violence toward his mother that he held in check:

He's very, very angry at hisself 'cause he stabbed his wife. He stabbed her and she dead. He's saying, "Oh, my God." He grabbed the knife and went over and stabbed her. She's just dead. He walks out the door and walks back in. He say, "What am I gonna do?" (What happens in the end?) He walks back in, put his hand back on, over his eyes.

Regarding this card, which is usually seen as a sexual scene, Jerome has described the hero as the murderer of the woman who was his wife. The hero has stabbed the woman with a knife—a murderously phallic instrument. The story of the stabbing was repeated three times. Aghast at what he had done and looking in disbelief at the act just committed, he felt very angry with himself for doing it. Still there she was—dead, "just dead." And he walked away from the scene of the violence, unable to confront the consequences of his aggression. When he walked back in, his ambivalence towards his mother—the dependence on her and the need to break the bond—was unresolved even after he had succeeded in getting rid of her by killing her. For after she was dead, he was lost, uncertain what or who would be the life support system for him. He asked, "What am I gonna do?" (without her?). He was alone and lost once again.

Distrust of Men

Although a great deal of Jerome's psychic energy was devoted to his ambivalent bond to his mother, a portion of his psychological world, albeit a much smaller part, involved men. Jerome had not had a strong, constant, and active father or father surrogate available to him. His recollection of his father was based on hearsay—the tale told by others that he said he hated to hear. The story was one of being neglected, mistreated, and abandoned by his father who did not and/or was not able to protect him from the physical abuse he suffered at the hands of his father's girl friend. At some point when he was a very young child, Jerome's father disappeared forever, never inquiring about his welfare even though he knew there had been difficulties between Jerome and his mother previously.

Jerome did not express any sense of loss about his father and the termination of their relationship. However, the enormous emotional pain he must have suffered as a result of being rejected, abandoned, and deserted by his father, though hidden, seemed to be present in some of his responses to the projective stimuli. He finished sentence completion item 66 with words about feelings experienced when people left him: "It hurts when *others go.*" Although in light of what we know about his continuing desire to be special with and close to his mother, a part of him might have actually been glad that his father was absent because this made for one less adult male for him to contend with and compete with for his mother's affections. However, in place of his father there was one man after another living with his mother over the years. Not only did these men displace him, they also failed to come to his rescue when his mother punished him severely.

> . . . when I was 14 she hit me in the head with a mustard jar and I had no place to run. I ran to her boyfriend and he, you know, he didn't do anything, he just laid in the bed, you know. But now I can stand up and do what, what I, I feel as though be right, you know.

This man, like his father, failed to protect him from the aggression directed toward him by a woman.

Jerome's response to TAT card 7BM, which shows a younger and older man together, provided evidence that Jerome had real and on-going struggles with adult males.

> Look like they gonna, getting ready to pull off a job. He's telling him what to do. He's just listening. This one saying everything to him, he's the brain. (The young one is the brain?) Yeah, the young one is the brain and the old man listening. And the old man said, "I'll get all the guns and everything. All the ammunition." The young one said, "I got the ride."

The story he produces described the two men as planning to execute a robbery, Jerome's stock-in-trade. The younger character was in charge and was seen as being "the brain." Although he may see himself as being cunning, all he could contribute was a car as a means of escape. The real power—the weapons—were possessed by the older man, the father figure. The older man, who is described by Jerome as having the guns and ammunition, was symbolically seen by him as having more penile and phallic power than he had. This raised the question concerning his own sense of masculinity and potency. In the story, the younger man had to rely on the older man to execute the "job," because he was not equipped to do it alone. He was not man enough. But he had fantasized that he provided the means of escape—the car and also that he was the one who had made the plans, something that the adult men around him always did in real life and whose authority he resented.

His sense of being mastered and controlled by older men was also demonstrated most strikingly in his response to TAT card 12M. The stimulus was of a younger man who was lying on a couch with the older man having his hand above the face of the younger man. Jerome produced the following story:

> He's playing a game, this guy right here. Putting his hands over his eyes. He wakes up and see him, asking him what he doing. He says, "I'm only playing, trying, trying to wave my hand over your eyes." (What happens in the end?) He lays back down, goes to sleep. And he still there having his hand. (Why was he waving his hand over the face like that?) Put him on top, put him on some type of a trance, a trance. (To do what?) To make him do what he want him to do. Hypnotize him.

The so-called game was not really a game at all. The older man was seen as attempting to gain power and control over the other, by placing him in a trance. By being in a trance or hypnotized he was at the mercy of the older man and was less able to resist being dominated against his will. It seemed as though Jerome saw adult males as being deceptive, cunning, and dishonest about their intentions toward him.

His negative view of men was further suggested as one hears his statements concerning his experiences at the two halfway houses he attended after his two respective incarcerations. At the Vindicate Society, the first postincarceration rehabilitation program, he stole a sum of money from the program's administrative office after being falsely accused of having a gun. He stated with braggadocia, "I beat that charge." Even though he was not found guilty he was required to withdraw from the program. His anger about being falsely accused by the male staff led him to stealing to get even.

Although he states that he was not fairly treated in being accused falsely, he admitted he failed to comply with many of the program's rules about smoking marijuana.

> I got high, had a good time, you know. You ain't suppose to get high in the program. But, you know, I got high anyway, did whatever I wan' to do. I said, "Fuck it, I'm here now," you know.

He became most angry when men did not treat him in the way he desired, but he was reluctant to respond to the rules that were established for him and others, leaving the impression that he had an insatiable need to rebel against those "man-made" rules of conduct that he perceived as restricting his actions. He described his feelings toward the men who ran the program as, "I didn't like the motherfuckers no way." It might be that he sees all adult men who restrict his path as being motherfuckers, men who have a close relationship with his mother that he wants but does not have.

Jerome's rebellious spirit and mistrust of men caused him additional problems. At the Vindicate Society, rules and structure were major facets of the rehabilitation program and there were physical means to ensure compliance. The male members of the staff were the enforcers. Jerome described their tactics:

> We use' to have boxing therapy there. They (the male counselors) would box you if you do something wrong. If you don't get the understanding the first time they'll box you, right, five or six people. Or a counselor would box with you. And I didn't like the way it was run.

Jerome did not like the way the program was conducted because he was frequently subjected to "boxing therapy" in the course of which he was physically beaten by one or more men. The counselors who administered this "therapeutic" treatment managed to increase his angry and negative feelings toward adult males.

Further difficulties with adult males occurred at the second halfway house where he lasted only a few months because of rule infractions and stealing.

> I: Jerome, you mentioned you left the Proof House program; why did you leave there?
>
> J: I don't know. I got on trouble.
>
> I: What happened?
>
> J: (Softly and almost apologetically) Stole something.
>
> I: What did you steal?
>
> J: Uhm, a rain, a rain jacket and got caught smoking reefer.
>
> I: When you look back over those incidents of stealing a raincoat and smoking reefer, what was going on those two times? First of all, why did you steal the coat? What was happening you stole the coat?
>
> J: It was raining, hard. And it was brand new and it was out there and I just took it (matter of factly). The dude came and asked me and I said 'Yeah.' He told the cops I stole it—they were parole officers—that I stole it. Then he caught me smoking reefer in my room. That was it . . . That's when I came down here (the Urban League).

Male adults in general were seen as being enforcers of standards of behavior. He knew that if he got out of line—whether they were cops, counselors, parole officers, or members of the National Guard—they were ready to put him away. This perception of men as enforcers was indicated in Jerome's response to TAT card 20.

> He look like a cop. He waiting this, he waiting on for somebody to do something, he waiting for do. And he have other friends that, on what's the job, whoever

gonna' to pull a job. Squatting to see if they gonna pull a job or not. And he walks around the corner, walks all the way around the corner, comes back to that same spot and looks at that same window. Saying, "Wonder when they're gonna' come out so that I can nab them."

Jerome seemed to be saying that he knew that he was inclined to "pull a job" (perform another act of thievery) and as soon as he did so, a cop would be there to arrest him. The police and all other males in authority were regarded by him as being his adversaries. Not only would they arrest him when he did something wrong, but they were always there to impede him from what he was attempting to do. His acts of aggression, most of which were larcenous in nature, were most frequently executed with a sense that no matter what he did he would be apprehended by some male in a role of authority. This was also indicated in his story to TAT card 18BM that showed a male being grabbed from the back by three hands.

He saying, "Please don't take me away. I done it, please don't take me away and put me in jail." He said, "Please don't take me away, I didn't mean to do it. Please forgive me." They take him away and is faint, and he faints. (What did he do?) Look like he committed a murder.

As he described his day-to-day life and his inner world via the projective instruments Jerome gave the impression that he may have performed many of his deviant acts for two purposes. The act of stealing and hurting someone were ways to get attention and to secure from men what he felt he could not get from his absent father and his mother's boyfriends. Being nabbed by an adult male in an authority role brought him in contact with the power that he would like to have possessed to establish and maintain control over his own life. This was illustrated in his description of being ejected from a federally funded and run job skills program that he attended after graduating from the Urban League training program.

I guess I'm the type of person who like to have fun, like to have fun. Then I got into this here trouble because, aah, I got caught smoking cigarettes. Like, ah, Bruce (name of counselor) asked me to put it out. I told him I'd put it out, right, and he came back and I had it lit again. He said, "You're suspended." So, aah, you know, I had left the program that Sunday night, right, and came back Monday night. And they told me I was suspended, that I couldn't come back on the grounds.

Although he saw men in authority as his adversaries, he may also have envied these men for what they were able to do. These same strong men were able to have sexual experiences with adult women, such as his mother, and he generally referred to them as "motherfuckers." Although hating these men for what they had done in various ways to displace him, at the same time he respected their ability to "make it" with older women—something that he was attempting to do. This indicated, on the one hand, a type of identification with the aggressor and, on the other hand, an ambivalence in his feelings towards adult males. What this combination led to was feelings of mistrust in all dealings with men, while being in constant awe of them.

The issue of mistrust of men came up at the end of one of the interviews and caught me by surprise. Jerome had previously told me on many occasions how much he looked forward to my visits with him. I had always appeared at the appointed time and thought I was gaining his trust in face of his previous difficulties with male adults. That he could not trust me after all the occasions I had not let him down—I had never broken a promise or betrayed his confidence in any way—served to further highlight the tremendous amount of deprivation he had suffered at the hands of all adults. Trusting anyone was very difficult for him; trusting a man seemed out of the question.

J: You know something? Honest, I didn't think you were gonna' come up (laughs).
I: (Incredulously) Oh, you didn't think I was going to come? (laughs)
J: No, I didn't (laughs).
I: I've always come before. Before you told me you knew I was coming because I've always come before. Now you tell me you didn't think I was going to come. Why were you so doubtful?
J: I don't know.
I: Share it with me. I want to hear this.
J: I was just doubtful. I said, "I don't think he's gonna' come."
I: When did you begin to doubt that I was going to come?
J: Yesterday. I said, "I don't think he's gonna' come."
I: I don't think you trust anybody. You don't trust anybody do you?
J: Myself (laughs).
I: Do you trust yourself? I think you feel that everybody is going to rip you off. People are not going to be honest with you, right?
J: Right, yeah.
I: So, everybody is out to screw you.
J: Yep. 'Cause when I think like that that's when I get very angry.
I: I'm out to screw you too, right? I'm not going to show up, "The cat is going to jam me up." So, you do not put yourself out there.
J: I told them you might come.
I: But you didn't believe it. Okay, I am glad that you can tell me that. It takes guts to do that, to tell the truth like that. What were you saying to yourself this morning when I told you I'd be here between ten thirty and eleven?
J: Now I'm gonna sleep. I just stayed in the bed (laughs).
I: You will not put yourself out there, right, you will not be vulnerable.
J: I stayed in bed and set my clock to lunch time and that's why I got up.
I: So you are saying, "If I don't begin to think about it I can't be hurt."

J: Right.

I: Let nobody know where you're coming from and you can't get hurt. That's a big part of how you operate. Let nobody know where you are coming from, right?

J: Right. You shouldn't. They might try to take advantage.

I: Okay, so that's what you're afraid of. I think that's a big, a very important thing about how you see things, Jerome. You feel everybody is going to fuck you. Right?

J: They're out to, you know.

I: You think they're out to, I hear you.

J: You know, well, like, yeah.

I: So, you try to fuck them first before they fuck you.

J: Nah, not really. It all depends upon who it is, you know.

For Jerome it was an established pattern to always protect himself from potential harm at the hands of an adult male. Rather than facing the disappointment of my not appearing as promised, he set his alarm clock to go off well after the appointed meeting time, but in time for him to go to lunch. Even if I did not appear, he would soothe himself by eating—a means of reducing his sense of loss and despair. Attempting to run away from the problem through sleep and gain substitute satisfaction through food suggested just how infantile and regressed he was.

In addition, Jerome's inability to make distinctions between the men he encountered and appreciate the history of individual relationships was a real and on-going problem for him. Men—all men—were placed in the category of being disappointers whom he must always watch out for and guard against. All adult males were persons who did not come to your rescue in times of need and who would leave you out in the cold. In his heart he wanted men, his father figures, to give him strength and to protect him from his mother, but he was afraid to trust them.

Heroes and Aspirations

Although Jerome found it difficult to trust the men who were a living part of his life, he seemed to have found some other men who held some importance for him. He spoke of seeing Dr. Martin Luther King, Jr. and Malcolm X as heroes. In his mind it was much safer to rely on a hero who was dead and distant than those father figures who were physically more available, but who had repeatedly let him down. Dr. King and Malcolm X gave their lives trying to help others help themselves. This was what his father figures had denied him. Even though he felt these men should be revered, Jerome had difficulty in fully recalling Dr. King's name.

He was more explicit and detailed in what he had to say about Malcolm X.

Stating that he had heard it said that members of the Nation of Islam had shot Malcolm X, he added that he wanted to find out whether this was the case or not. It may be that this quest resonated with his wanting to know the whereabouts and the history of his own father whom he had not seen since the day he abandoned him on the steps of his mother's home.

Another feature of Jerome's fantasy life was that of becoming a truck driver. Saying he would like to travel "all over," he was without any real sense of a particular destination or direction, but he felt there was a great deal for him to see and experience. As he continued to talk about traveling, he thought it might be nice to visit the Bahamas, Florida, and Africa. His desire to travel might be interpreted as his means of finally escaping from his mother and all the problems he associated with her. But the far-off places he mentioned also suggested the notion of a quest for knowledge about himself, his family, and his roots. Traveling might have represented his way of looking for his father and at the same time finding himself. As it stood, he had little or no information concerning his family—he knew nothing at all about his father and very little about his mother and her background. When he asked the question posed by many adolescents, "Who am I?" the answer could contain no more than vague and piecemeal images because his life had been so unstable, broken, clouded, and poorly defined.

Jerome articulated quite explicitly some of the goals he strove for. These were autonomy and separation and a stable home life such as he had never experienced.

> I would like, you know, really, I would like to have my own place, just to cool out, just to know I had it. But I'm waiting for that particular date, 'cause, like, I know right now, you know, I don't care how much I talk, I know I gonna have what I want eventually. I gonna have it, you know, it might take me a little while, but I'm gonna have what I want.
>
> I: That is important to you, having what you want.
> J: Yeah! That's very important to me. And plus I have other people helping me, too. But I can't always depend on their hope; I got to depend on my hope, you know. Because they ain't out here for me, I'm out here for myself.
> I: What do you want to accomplish? What do you want for yourself?
> J: I want to be a truck driver. I want to have my own house. I want to get married, I want to have some kids. I just wanna' cool out, you know. I wanna stay satisfied with myself, stay, stay satisfied with myself, you know.

So far Jerome had been anything but satisfied with himself and his life situation. His use of the "cool out" indicated that his life up to this time had been very heated and difficult and he wished to have a permanent reprieve from the firing lines of his past since birth. Blaming his mother for the hardships and difficult times encountered by him and his siblings, what he was hoping for in starting a new life was very different from what he and his family had lived. The picture he drew of what he wanted could best be described as stability. He would like to turn a new page of his life that he would live on his own.

J: She ain't treat us right.
I: None of you?
J: Not all of us. My sister left when she was young. I don't know how old she was when she left. But my sister drinks, she drinks galore, she drinks, boy, oh man! She just drinks. She drinks so much I had to take a drink. She drinks. And her husband does drugs. My other sister is on welfare to support her husband and she has six girls, you know. I say, "Damn, I don't want to have no type of life like they living right now. I want to have my own life, the way I want to have it,' you know."
I: You have a brother, too.
J: Yeah, George.
I: Where is George?
J: He stay with another dude. Well, he's gay. And I didn't like the point he staying with him, but at least he had some place to stay and I don't. So, he doing better than me, you know.
I: Sounds as though things have been difficult for a long time.
J: Yeah, I had been, but I'm straggling to become something.

The search and quest for a haven in the form of a home reflected the degree of deprivation that Jerome has undergone. Even his brother who was homosexual was better off than he was because at least he had a place to live. To have a place of his own—something most people take for granted—was what he was now striving for. His intense wish to realize his goal was vividly described in his response to TAT card 17, which depicts a male figure climbing a rope.

Oh, he's trying to make it to his goal. Boy, he's climbing that rope. Climbing it, he's climbing it. He's going back to the bottom, he's racing again. He goes up to the top. He says, "I gonna' finally make that reach. I gonna finally make peak, where I want to go, what I want to do. I'm gonna' get up there." He know he gonna make it, he know, he look on, he has the look on his face saying, "I'm gonna make it. I'm gonna' make it."

Self-Doubts

Although Jerome wanted to be as dedicated and successful as the man in the story, in the past many if not all of his attempts would backfire on him. So much of the time he had wound up being self-destructive in his attempts to climb out of the morass he was in. This was aptly illustrated in his discussion of a conversation he had with a police officer after being arrested for stealing from a woman.

Your mother talk to the people and everything and Mrs. Thomas (the Urban League counselor) is supposed to be coming down.' The policeman from East Orange jail knew Mrs. Thomas—he went to church with her and everything, in Newark, right, on Broad Street. So, he said, "Don't worry about it. I know she's coming down." right. "I know she'll be able to get you out of it," right. I said, "Thank you very much," you know. He said, "Just spend," you know, "a couple days in jail and everything will be all right." Otherwise I would have been pissed off. "I just don't want to be in here." If he didn't say that, I would have done something worse than that.

I: What would you have done?

J: I don't know—hit myself, hurt myself or something. I would have tried to cut myself. I just hate being confined, you know.

I: What do you think you would have accomplished by hurting yourself?

J: Nothing, but I just didn't want to be in jail.

I: Okay, so by cutting yourself what did you hope would happen then?

J: I wouldn't solve nothing.

I: But you were telling yourself what would have happened. What do you think would have happened if you cut yourself? How would they have treated you there if you had cut yourself?

J: They would put me in the hospital.

I: So, that was your way of getting out of jail.

J: Yep. They would have taken me to, aah, what you call it; I forgot what you call it, Overbrook.

I: You mean the psychiatric hospital (incredulously)?

J: Yeah.

I: You mean that you wanted them to think you were crazy?

J: Yeah, but I wouldn't let them put needles in my head.

This interchange with Jerome demonstrated the way he thought of acting when confronting some difficulty such as confinement. He would think of escaping from a situation and wind up putting himself in greater jeopardy. He knew full well what the consequences of his behavior would be—that he would be sent to a psychiatric hospital. Such acts of self-destruction would only lead to a change of venue of his place of incarceration and more personal pain—hardly a preferable solution to his plight. Getting out of a tight spot (jail) would land him in another worse one (psychiatric hospital).

What was not changed were the perceptions of him by others as being out of control, incompetent, and/or sick. Instead of looking independent and autonomous in the way he wished to appear, he was seen in each situation as being unable to care for himself. In the imprisonment he referred to he controlled himself only because he knew his mother and Mrs. Thomas were coming to get him out of jail. Otherwise his own way of getting out was to consider hurting himself so that he would be treated as a mental patient. Feeling trapped, the only person he could strike out at was himself. His anger was inflicted on himself. Such thoughts of self-attack indicated that deep inside he blamed himself for many of his difficulties. When he was unable to lash out at others he considered resorting to masochism.

This sense that he was unable to fully pull off his attempt at independence and separation was also illuminated in his response to TAT card 14, which depicts a male figure sitting in the dark.

> Look like he's trying to get out of a dark house. Trying to get to the light. He finally gets to the light and say, "Why not. It's fun being in the dark," and goes back in.

Deep down inside of himself Jerome felt he could not really make it on his own. He would remain in his emotional and physical darkness because that was all he really knew. Because he could not handle the light of day, he could deny it was better out there and retreat to the darkness. Contrary to what he said about it being fun the reason he actually remained in the dark was that it was familiar to him and less threatening than the demands of freedom and independence.

Jerome's concerns and doubts about his ability to make it in the larger world were also contained in the description he gave of his drawing for the male segment of the Draw-A-Person projective exercise. Looking at the figure he had drawn he said that the male "ain't made right" and he "sure don't look like a man."

I: The first figure you said is a man. Tell me about that person.
J: Tell you about him?
I: Yeah.
J: Ain't nothing to tell. All right, I know I draw him. He don't look like a man everybody else would draw.
I: Your man is different than everybody else would draw?

FIGURE 1.   Jerome's First Drawing for the Draw-A-Person Test.

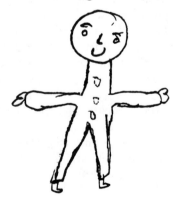

J: (Laughs) I draw him a different way. Head ain't made right, nose suppose be on the side. I'm suppose to be drawing a man, his nose suppose to be on the side. He needs more stuff done to him.

I: What does he need done to him?

J: A hat probably, clothes. He still don't look like a man.

I: What's missing?

J: Arms, the legs, the way his body moves, I mean the way I made the body. His eyes, ears, and his mouth. If you really gonna draw a picture you should put it sideways so that you can see one ear, you're not suppose to see the other ear.

I: Anything else you want to change about him?

J: His feet. That's it.

The drawing provided data for the impression that Jerome saw himself as highly vulnerable to the various forces and people that surrounded him. The self-disclosing figure Jerome drew positioned himself as suspended in midair devoid of physical (and psychological) supports. The figure's upper and lower extremities were extended as if to indicate that he had given up and was unable to protect himself. Even though the figure was drawn with its legs apart there was no sign of him having a penis, an indication of his lack of masculinity and personal potency. The garment the figure was wearing looked like an infant's one-piece suit with decorative balls. It might be that the only balls (gonads) he felt he had were on the article of clothing. Take the unisex garment away and he was essentially castrated. The only sense of power seen in his drawing was the phallic shape of the feet. Other signs of underdevelopment were seen in his drawing of the hands that were mittenlike with a thumb and a web for the remaining fingers, suggesting his lack of dexterity to *man*ually operate and engineer his world. In comparison with the size of the paper on which it was drawn, the figure was small, hopeless, aloft, and about to surrender. These features of his drawing suggested that Jerome saw himself as being more like a baby than a man.

In fact, the figure he drew was not a complete man because he "needs stuff done to him." By securing a hat and some clothing it was his hope that he will *look* more like a man. But there were all kinds of body parts he would want to change in the way he drew the figure. When he said, "Don't look like a man everybody else would draw," he acknowledged that deep within himself he felt he was not a man that anyone would recognize as a man. Sensing that he was not at all what he wanted to appear to the world, he knew that he was different, deficient, and not what people saw him as being. Beneath all the supposed physical strength he was a very young, frightened, ungrounded, and immature baby. Even the clothing that he used to "cover" himself could best be described as babyish.

Similar doubts Jerome entertained about his ability to be an adult male who was in control of his life were seen in his response to TAT card 1. This stimulus showed a young boy sitting at a desk with a violin in front of him. Jerome described the picture in these words:

> He want to learn how to play the, he looking at it. He say "Well, I want to learn how to play, how, the violin." He wants to know if it's hard to play. And he's thinking about picking it up. That's it. (What happens at the end?) At the end? (Yeah.) He get disgusted with hisself because he can't play it. He wish he could play it.

As was true in his story of the boy with the violin he did not have the courage to pick up the bow, which is a condensed symbol of his general sense of being incompetent to achieve anything. "He get disgusted with hisself" because he feared he would not be able to play the role of a man.

OVERVIEW: JEROME'S PSYCHOLOGICAL WORLD

Jerome's behavior becomes understandable once it is realized that there has been a certain kind of developmental failure—that he has experienced disturbances in the processes of separation and individuation (Kohut, 1971). On the threshold of manhood Jerome arrived at the age of 18 being preoccupied with his ambivalent feelings towards his mother—ill-equipped to let go of his infantile yearning to be physically and emotionally attached to her and at the same time desiring to be independent of her, a person in his own right. There were clear signs that he was struggling, however ineffectively and counterproductively, to free himself of his dependence on her.

The form that Jerome's delinquency takes is petty thievery. His "thing," as he calls it, is purse snatching. But he does not attack people when he grabs their possessions. Not a mugger, Jerome is not physically aggressive while he robs them. Some of his earliest acts of delinquency involved taking money from his mother's pocketbook when it was lying around the apartment. Later he widened the scope of his victims to include purse snatching from other women and to a few instances of breaking and entering. By now he is skilled at the practice of this antisocial activity, but it must not be forgotten that there was a first time. As Winnicott (1973) reminds us, "There was a beginning and at the beginning there was an illness, and the boy or girl becomes a deprived child. In other words there is sense in what once happened." The sense in what once happened and has continued to happen to Jerome may provide the basis for illuminating the relationship between the impairments in his psychological development and his delinquent behavior.

Jerome may be best described as a baby who is occupying the body of a strong, even virile, young man. Although he appears to have grown and thrived physically, the same cannot be said for his emotional development. There is much about him that suggests an arrest in the development of the structure of his world (Stolorow & Lachman, 1980). Whatever special vulnerability to impediments in his growth may have been due to Jerome's constitutional endowments is unknown. But certainly many of the difficulties Jerome encountered in the process of the development of a self can be attributed to the quality of the interaction between Jerome and his caretakers from infancy on (Mahler, Pine, & Bergman, 1975) and particularly the discontinuous and dissonant interaction with his mother and mother substitutes and their apparently neglectful and sometimes abusive behavior towards him (Winnicott, 1971). Handed back and forth between two women who did not want to mother him—from house to house, family to family, and later from one penal institution to another and from this job skills program to that training project, Jerome never knew the security of continuous mothering or the stability of a permanent home. A healthy, vital, cohesive self has little chance to develop under these conditions. Without a certain steadiness in relationships and little of the empathy, affirmation, and mirroring a child needs from his caretakers, Jerome possesses a stunted self that has hardly come into its own at all (Kohut, 1971, 1977). His growth was dwarfed by the shattering impact of negligence in caring for him and injuries inflicted on his body and emotional life.

Despite his persistent pattern of stealing from his mother and others, in his fantasy life Jerome pictures himself as having an idealized, warm, protective, and loving relationship with the mother he robs—a relationship that is reminiscent of the closeness of an infant with his mother. In fact, Jerome openly expresses the desire to sleep in her bed and to have an exclusive call on her love, not to be shared with the other men in her life. Not only does he want to cut the other objects of her attention and sexual intimacy out of her life, but he desires to be, in his own words, "a part" of her in the manner of the symbiotic intertwining of mother and baby. The very expression of the desired relationship with his mother as being not simply "with" her but rather as being "a part" of her brings to mind those earliest months of life when an infant does not distinguish his body from his caretakers— when he has not developed a psychological existence separate from the mother's. In Winnicott's (1971) view, when the mother presents her breast to the infant, "Psychologically the infant takes from a breast that is part of the infant, and the mother gives milk to an infant that is part of herself" (p. 12). When the mothering is "good enough," as Winnicott goes on to postulate,

The mother, at the beginning, by an almost 100% adaptation affords the infant the opportunity for the *illusion* that her breast is part of the infant. It is, as it were, under the baby's magical control. The same can be said in terms of infant care in general. (p. 11)

In Jerome's case there is little doubt that he lacked a "good-enough mother"—
one who made these adaptations to his demands with the "easy and unresented
preoccupation" with him that is required for a healthy start in life. It was not a
matter of his mother's lack of education and some kind of special knowledge
about child rearing, for "success in infant care depends on the fact of devotion,
not on cleverness or intellectual enlightenment."

To understand the context of Jerome's delinquent behavior it is important to
realize how far short of making an "100% adaptation" to his initial needs his
natural mother and mother surrogate fell. The situation was that Jerome was
never central to either of their lives at the time he was in their care. They failed
to give him even a reasonable fraction of the kind of total preoccupation and
devotion he needed because they had pressing agendas of their own, ones that
had no place for him except as a burden. In fact, they resented having to take the
time to take care of him. His natural mother (who did not want to keep him)
gave him over to his father. After being shipped to his father's house he was put
in the hands of his father's girl friend who abused him physically. Subsequently
his father deposited him once again with his natural mother who took him back
reluctantly, always had "trouble" rearing him, and beat him frequently.

It can be assumed that Jerome never experienced good enough mothering.
He was not only neglected but he was abused. It seems as though he had learned
at a very early age that the only way he could gain anything from his mother—
either affection or even attention—would be by taking it from her. Symbolically
and actually he took from his mother what she had not given him as an infant
and would not give to him freely later on—herself. He wanted both to *take* a
part of her and *be* a part of her.

Although Jerome could get attention from his mother by stealing from her
and others, it was not a very satisfying way of gaining her attention because it
made her angry. His continued acts of stealing, then, can be seen as a series of
restitutive acts, attempting to recreate the lost era when what he wanted as an
infant should have been granted by a good enough mother. Because Jerome
thought of himself, as he put it, as "a part" of his mother, her possessions were
considered his and he took them from her quite freely. He stole from her what
he thought was due him and she had failed to give him. From his infantile view
this consisted of anything that was hers—her things, representing symbolically
to him her love and undivided devotion, which she was and is unwilling to give
to him voluntarily.

Because Jerome's mother had put him out on his own at age 16, before he
was ready psychologically to separate himself from him, he continues to search
for an idealized mother–infant closeness with other mother figures, especially
with women in the helping professions. Wishing to create a relationship with
these older women of the kind he actually desires with his mother, he goes from
one to the next looking for a Good Mother who will make him the central focus
of her life. Actually he is hungry for that *one* perfect relationship with the good

or "real mother" who will never deny him anything. When the women who have tried to help him have failed him by turning down the most whimsical of his requests, he re-experiences the shattering trauma of the disappointments inflicted upon him during his development. He strikes back by stealing from the mother substitutes who like his own mother do not respond to his cries for nurturing. Jerome's form of delinquency—his stealing—is rooted in his infant experiences in still another way. Because his caretakers deprived him of the illusion of omnipotence, which most children experience from having their mothers respond to their every demand, he lacked the basis for the gradual disillusionment during the process of being weaned to learn how to tolerate frustration and deal with reality. Unless from the beginning the mother adapts almost exactly to the infant's demands, "it is not possible for the infant to begin to develop a capacity to experience a relationship to external reality, or even to form a conception of external reality" (Winnicott, 1971, p. 14).

Jerome's poor grasp of reality is frequently reflected in the way he carries out his delinquent acts. It seems as if he cannot resist the impulse to steal from anyone who has what he wants at any particular moment, whether the person happens to be his benefactor or an utter stranger. His impulsive drive system tends to govern his behavior to such an extent that he usually does not consider the possible consequences of his actions. He justified one act of thievery—stealing a raincoat—by stating that it was raining and he did not want to get wet. That the coat did not belong to him was immaterial. The idea of asking to borrow the coat temporarily did not occur to him. His stealing is a symptom of the disturbance in making the transition from omnipotence to reality (Winnicott, 1971).

Jerome commits his delinquent acts with an astonishing lack of foresight for the possible negative consequences for himself. This seems to stem partly from his truncated perception of time. All that counts is what is taking place at the very instant in question. Consequently, he does not concern himself with the history of his relationships nor does he experience himself as extended into the future. Within him there is a lack of personal continuity, making him unable to align and affiliate himself with anyone or anything in an on-going cooperative way except in the most tenuous degree. As a result he risks his all in his relationships at the point of each infraction and deviant act. This pattern of stealing reflects Jerome's failure to develop a temporal self that can postpone instant gratification for the sake of some future benefits.

Jerome does not have the sense of self that allows him to shrug off a frustrating event (Stolorow & Lachman, 1980). The slightest hurt is experienced as a mortal blow, which must be avenged, especially when he is frustrated by a maternal figure. Having a very high standard of performance for the good mother he expects her to supply everything he wants. When this does not occur, Jerome fails to recall those times that the person occupying the role of the maternal object had helped him in the past. Any woman who attempts to assist him is almost certain to be an eventual recipient of his wrath and rage because he can never be fully content with her responses to him. Damaged by the early psychological deprivations suffered at the hands of his mothers, Jerome is forever on the alert to protect himself from the possible and probable harm he sees lurking in his involvements with all women. His revenge takes the form of stealing from them.

At the same time Jerome seems to have a need to fancy himself as being a ladies' man who "can get over" on women. Harboring this conception of himself along with angry and aggressive feelings toward women, it is not out of the question that Jerome could become a pimp or a rapist. Each of these forms of male behavior involves taking advantage of, exploiting, and/or abusing women for emotional and financial gain. It is thought by many that both the pimp and the rapist are men who actually hate women and feel proud of themselves when they are subjugating women. There is psychic potential for Jerome to act out his aggressive feelings toward women in either of these two roles that denigrate and deprecate females.

The absence of his father during practically all his life undoubtedly was significant in Jerome's psychological development. Being without this needed model, Jerome had no grown man to identify with. He certainly did not admire this man who had deserted him. In fact, he barely mentioned anything about him, except his distress over the fact that his father had allowed his girl friend to beat him. Nor did Jerome fantasize about having an absent father who actually cared about him very much and really did not abandon him after all. His mother's boyfriends who might have served as father substitutes or at least as male role models never seemed to become involved with Jerome in meaningful ways. Although Jerome was outspokenly jealous of them and hated them intensely—and indeed was in competition with them for his mother—the relationships between them and himself apparently were so tenuous that he could not, or at least did not, use them as father figures in the oedipal struggle. Possibly this was because these rivals for his mother's love were so close to his own age, more like brothers than fathers. In any case, Jerome was enormously distrustful of men. He had an established pattern for protecting himself from potential harm at the hands of adult males whom he placed in the category of disappointers and enforcers of rules he was disinclined to obey.

In an attempt to formulate a theory for the etiology of delinquency that derives "to some extent from the general body of understanding that has come through psychoanalysis," Winnicott proposes that children's delinquent acts are linked inherently with deprivation. In the case of theft, there is a failure of the relationship between the small child and the mother. Winnicott (1973) states: It is the mother who

> enables the child creatively to find objects. . . . When this fails the child has lost contact with objects. . . . At the moment of hope the child reaches out and steals

an object. This is a compulsive act and the child does not know why he or she does it. Often the child feels mad because of having a compulsion to do something without knowing why. Naturally the fountain pen stolen from Woolworth's is not satisfactory; it is not the object that was being sought, and *in any case the child is looking for the capacity to find, not for an object.* Nevertheless there may be some satisfaction belonging to what is done at the moment of hope. (p. 366)

If the act of stealing is a moment of hope, what is its meaning to the child? According to Winnicott, the child is sending a signal—an S.O.S.—in an attempt to let significant others know that something is awry and in the hope that parents or other adults will recognize the message about feeling deprived and rescue him from the intense suffering he feels. This happens to children everywhere, even to those brought up in caring homes. Such a child may be responding to some relatively moderate sort of deprivation and if the parents react with understanding and some indulgence the child will weather the storm and come through the difficulty in good psychological shape. He may steal again but probably only on rare occasions.

At the other extreme there is the adolescent like Jerome whose early acts of stealing are not recognized as cries for help. Instead he is punished and forced to give logical explanations for his misbehavior. Gradually the stealing becomes compulsive, and its meaning in the life of the adolescent is lost. In Jerome's case it is clear that his antisocial behavior is rooted in the shattering events of his early psychological history, and his acts of stealing are distress signals that have gone unheeded.

3

The Case
of Pete

The many difficulties encountered by black inner-city youth when they attempt
to individuate and separate from parental ties may serve as keys to an understanding of their delinquent behavior. A boy's experiences in infancy and adolescence
may complicate his efforts to break the maternal bond and cultivate his emerging self. For Pete and many ghetto youth, the normal transition from childhood
to adulthood is more traumatic because of serious disruptions in their early and
later relationships with primary others—family members whose responses to
them have been seriously distorted in various degrees by the stresses engendered
in the social context of the black ghetto. For the boy who becomes delinquent, it
may well be that he becomes engaged in antisocial behavior more easily because
of these emotional ruptures and deprivations that have affected his relationships
with his parents. It is almost as if the boy is propelled into satisfying some
enormous needs that have not been attended to for most of his life. Unfortunately,
the delinquent acts often mask the boy's underlying problems rather than
providing an effective means of aiding his psychological growth.

PETE: HIS SELF–PRESENTATION

Due to his small size, Pete did not look his age. Although 17 years old, he was
only 5 feet tall and weighed around 115 pounds. However, he was sturdily
built—the partly opened shirt of his khaki uniform revealed a fairly muscular
chest. When he put his right hand to his mouth to retrieve his cigarette, the
large number of scars across his knuckles were noticeable. There were similar
scars and signs of old bruises on his left hand—the markings of a fighter.

Taking quick puffs from his cigarettes, Pete was apprehensive at the outset of
the interviews. His manner was warm and pleasant but he smiled nervously,

asking politely for permission to smoke. After checking out the interviewer, very carefully, he eventually relaxed when he learned that the interviews would be taped and used for research and not by the penal facility or the court.

Pete's Personal History

Pete was the middle child of a family of five boys. The two older siblings (20 and 19 years old) were the sons of a man whom Pete had never known. Pete and his younger brother (14 years old) were the children of another man whom Pete always referred to as his father. The youngest brother who was 9 years old was fathered by the man currently living with his mother.

> Like, like, me and my brother, right, we got the same father. And, uhm, my two oldest brothers, they got the same father and my little brother, he got a different father, you know. My little brother's father, that is my stepfather. Yeah, that, I don't understand that, we all have different fathers, you know . . . seem like she can't stay with one man.

Pete's parents were separated and subsequently the man Pete referred to as his "stepfather" moved in and lived with the family. After the separation Pete's father would come back to visit him, but because fights between his father and stepfather often ensued, his father eventually discontinued the visits and stopped seeing him completely.

Pete's mother worked long hours at a state psychiatric hospital as a licensed practical nurse. Although the eldest son still lived at home, he had a job to go to early in the morning, so at around age 13, Pete was given the responsibility of taking care of the two younger boys and maintaining the household. He had to see that his brothers were dressed, fed, and off to school before he left the house himself—and he usually walked the youngest to school.

> Like my mother goes to work . . . you know. I clean up the whole house thinking I got everything done when she come back, you know, so like when she come from work I can go out. But, you know, seem like everything will be straight, you know, she'll find something wrong or something . . . I be thinking I clean everything. My little brother and them, the one who is 14, like to be playing around the house. I still go behind them and clean it up so she won't have nothing to say when she come home. But it seem like something is wrong, she always finds something wrong.

There was one member of the family, his older brother, Ray, who Pete thought really understood him and recognized what life was like for him at home.

It is only one of my brothers who, he knows, he sees my problem, you know. He know that my mother be too hard on me. My second oldest brother, he know . . . He is in the army. He even told my mother one time that she, you know, was kinda' too hard on me.

Pete spoke very positively about his relationships with people outside his family. He frequently talked about the parties he attended with his friends and bragged a good deal about his success with girls. One of these girls who was named Gloria became his steady girl friend—he had gone with her for 4 years. She was the mother of his 3-year-old son.

Pete's other major involvement outside the family was with a street gang. The motto of the group was the same as that of the Three Musketeers (although he did not associate the two): "One for all, all for one."

They are alright. They, they are good friends. They, if you're in trouble and somebody jumping you or something, they, all you got to do is, you know, go get them, you know. And the person jumping you is really gonna' get it, they're gonna' get them . . . They are good friends . . . they're good people.

The other members of the gang were big and aggressive—they liked "to do wild things, like fighting. They're crazy, wild." Talking about his own reasons for fighting, Pete explained: "It's because I'm short, you know, and they are a lot of big boys. I guess I had to get a reputation so that they would know me. That's how I be thinking sometimes. I'd say, 'I wish I wasn't short.' "

Pete engaged in many street fights with his "boys." Besides the fighting, the gang also committed many felonies, most of which were "B and E's," breaking and entering offenses. They used much of the money they stole to buy marijuana, a drug frequently used by Pete. Although some of the gang members indulged in hard drugs, Pete declined their invitations to join them.

Much of Pete's early deviant behavior was truancy from school and running away from home—and staying away for a number of days. But when he became a part of the gang, he began to engage in fighting, stealing, vandalism, and breaking and entering other people's property. His current incarceration was for stealing a coat and 12 cents from a 12-year-old boy, an act he performed with one of his fellow gang members. His first arrest (which occurred when he was 14) was for malicious damage of a woman's property. He described what happened:

P: This lady, you know, she threw some hot water on me. So I bust her windows in her house and car windows and flattened her tires and all.
I: Why did she throw the water on you?
P: Because I was fighting her son. I was beating him up and she threw some hot water on me. And then I got mad and just went and got a lot of my boys and all

of us just grab rocks and stuff. Was throwing them through the windows and busting the car windows. Then she press charges on me of malicious damage.

It was not a rare occasion for Pete to become involved in physical combat. In fact, he had been arrested quite a number of times following various altercations with people who he thought had insulted him in some minor way. The behavior that had led to Pete's first arrest was characteristic of him. He described what had triggered this fight:

I: So, what was the fight all about?
P: About bumping, I think I bumped into him or he bumped into me or something, you know. I know he had something in his hand that fell out of his hand, you know. He said, "Damn, why don't you watch where you're going." I said, "It wasn't my fault." Then he said, "You knocked my shit out of my hand." I said, "And bump that," and then I went to walk. He said, "What you want to do," and all that kind of stuff. I said, "Man, get out of my face." He was coming at my face pointing. I just mushed him and told him not to point at my face. Then we just started fighting. Then his mother ran out there and say, "You better beat his," you know, "beat his ass," you know. And I was beating him up and I think she was going, you know, to get a belt or something, you know, to beat his ass. But she came out with some water, you know, some hot water and threw it on me.
I: Did you get burned?
P: A little bit. Aah, aah, it was, like, a little bit on my arm. A little bit, somewhere up here (on his upper left arm). A little bit, but I had on this, on this, like, a hood, one of them sweatsuit hoods. It just burned me a little bit, I know it was hot. I said, "I'm gonna' get you for that." Then she took her son, and took him in the house and slammed the door. I got mad 'cause I was all wet and went, went and got some of my friends. Then we waited for a while 'til it got a little dark. I said, told everybody to get a lot of rocks. Got a lot of rocks and bust the windows.

From this account it is apparent that Pete's determination to get revenge did not arise solely from the physical injury he suffered. Pete experienced such incidents as radical assaults upon his own masculine self and was as a result prone to react in an extreme and violent fashion. As will be documented at length in the later sections, his vulnerability to these narcissistic insults was related to a sense of pervasive loneliness and ambivalence about defining an independent identity. In the material that follows, an attempt is made to gain understanding of Pete's reactions and experiences through an examination of the meaning of his delinquent acts in the context of his psychological world as a whole.

PETE'S INNER WORLD

Pete's most cherished memories were of the days before his parents' separation, when his own father was still at home and the family was together.

> Like, they uhm, at night, you know we be sitting, like in my mother's and father's room on my mother's and father's bed, you know. We all used to be in there. They be lying on the bed watching TV, too, you know. 'Cause every, we used to stay up 'till he come home. He used to always bring something home to us, you know, to eat, watch TV, you know. We in there and my mother would make like she was tired, you know. If she wasn't tired we would squeeze her or doing something. My mother was like that. She used to be, seem like she used to always be happy, you know, together, but. I used to always talk to her and all that.

Paradise Lost

The departure of his father from what Pete recalled as a blissfully happy, almost magically perfect family circle, seemed to have created for him a traumatic void—a loss that was a recurring theme in every conversation. The breakup of his parents was repeatedly referred to but the facts surrounding it were vague and often inaccurate. He did not even come close to remembering what age he was when his father left. At first stating that he had been 12 years old, he was surprised to learn that he was only 8 years old at the time it happened.

Unlike many youngsters who are at least somewhat aware of their parents' difficulties through the frequency and intensity of their quarrels, Pete did not recall having any such warnings. When he was informed one day by his mother that his father would not be at home any more, he was taken by surprise. His mother had refused to give him any explanation for the breakup and Pete himself could not formulate any interpretation of the events even when pressed to do so.

I: What do you think happened between your parents all of a sudden? Seems as though they were cooperating and everything was mellow and cool for them, or had there been problems before?

P: No problems that I know of. I thought everything was alright.

I: It must have been like a shock to you. How did you get notified that they were breaking up?

P: I don't know. I know aah, she said she would be seeing him no more . . . I said, "Why not?" and she said, "Something, never mind," you know. That's all, you know, she left me unknown, you know. I know nothing about why they broke up.

I: You still don't have any idea at all what happened?

P: She never told me.

I: Did you ask her what went on?

P: Yeah, I asked her. I asked her a couple times. I said, "Ma, why you, why you and daddy broke up?" She paid it no mind . . . So I don't really know."

The person who had been at the center of his small world was gone and all the sunshine went out of his life: "I guess since he left, I, you know, I didn't care. I didn't want him to leave you know." When pressed, he said he thought it was his mother's fault that his father was no longer present. He wondered why his mother could not stay with just one man—she had children by three different men.

THE IDEALIZED FATHER

Sensing that his childhood was a Paradise Lost, Pete clung tenaciously to an image of the perfection of those early times and a picture of a father who was always loving and generous to him.

But I know my father used to talk to me. Take me, he used to always take me to White Castle. I remember that, I know that. He used to always take me out. When I see him pull up in front of the house I just grab my coat and run downstairs. And I ask him to take me somewhere, he take me straight to White Castle, buy a lot of hamburgers and come back to the house, you know, and have a lot of hamburgers, you know. Me and my brothers would eat them . . . If my stepfather pulled up in front of the house, I don't even budge, just lay right in my bed. I ain't running downstairs.

In this and many other accounts of being with his father Pete painted a picture of a special and nurturant relationship in which he never experienced disappointment or neglect. There was, in Pete's view, or at least in what he would or could express openly, nothing about his father he would think of criticizing—and Pete at no time uttered a breath of criticism of him, even though his father had not been in touch with him since he was 8 years old and had failed to visit him or telephone him while he was in prison.

Outwardly Pete's identification with his idealized father remained untarnished by what had happened since his departure from the home. Apparently he even looked something like his father. He remarked with rueful pride that his mother sometimes mentioned angrily how much he resembled his father, a possible reason, in Pete's view, for the bad treatment he received at her hands after his father left. "I know she told me when I wear those hats, I look just like him. So maybe because she see me like him or something like that. She see me; I picture her; I picture her of him or something." Everything had gone downhill for Pete after "he left":

He (his "stepfather") didn't move right in after they, he (his father) left, you know. It took some time. I don't know how long it took, he didn't move in right after he left. After that I started.

I: You started getting into trouble after that? So, maybe you were very young when you started getting into trouble, you were 8 maybe?

P: I don't really know, but I know after he left I know, I did, I know, right after he started, after he left, you know, he wasn't coming in, a different man was coming in. I just started getting into trouble.

I: How did you feel about this man coming in the house and taking your father's place?

P: I didn't like him. Plus my mother told me I had to call him daddy. He liked us to call him daddy, you know. I was saying to myself, "He ain't never hear that come out my mouth."

Although Pete never previously and openly ventured an explanation for the breakup of his parents, he—like many young children of divorced parents—may have blamed himself for it. Possible support for this can be found in his responses to the Thematic Apperception Test. In his story about TAT card 7BM, the younger man was being given some "bad news" by the older man to whom he replied, "Father, I'm sorry for what happened. But it wasn't my fault. Please understand." The story in full was as follows:

Two man having a conversation. He must be telling him some bad news, 'cause the expression on his face. (Who is telling who bad news?) This man right here, he must be telling him some bad news. (So the older man is telling the younger man bad news?) Yeah. He must be telling him some bad news, by the expression on the face, the way he looking. I'll just make up a story. he telling him some bad news and he saying, "Why did it have to happen to me? What did I do wrongly? Oh, Lord, please forgive me for what I did. Please try to understand me. Father, I'm sorry for what happened. But it wasn't my fault. Please understand."

In Pete's case, the "bad news" of his young life was that his father had forsaken him without any warning or explanation. Even today, so many years after the traumatic rupture of the harmonious family circle, Pete still did not know what actually went wrong between his parents and between his father and himself. The thought that he himself might have done something to cause the trouble between his parents was unbearable. Possibly he was the guilty one. In the story the young man pleaded for explanation and forgiveness at the same time, "What did I do wrongly? Oh, Lord, please forgive me for what I did." Asserting on the one hand that it was his fault, he continued to beg for understanding and forgiveness for his guilty role in the bad news his father had broken to him. His innocent bewilderment echoed the cry of Jesus from the cross, "My God, why hast Thou forsaken me?"

Although Pete kept his idealized image of his father intact in this story, his response to card 8BM might be interpreted as a reflection of some more negative feelings about his father's absence from the home. Not having his father present, Pete had found himself unprotected from the hostile elements in his environment. In his story to TAT card 8BM, the older male figure, a paternal figure, admitted that he was at fault for not listening to the younger male, who had been shot. In this story it was the older figure who asked for the younger one's forgiveness as he lay dying.

> The boy wondering, the man said, "Boy, watch it." This had to happen to him at a young age. That things are just, that things were just beginning to happen. It had to happen. "If I would have listen it never would have happened to him. But I just wouldn't listen. Maybe he wouldn't gotten shot if I would've listen, if I would've listen to him. No, I had to do it anyway. No, I had to do it, had to do it anyway. Hope you will forgive me. Please let him live. It's all my fault what happened to him." (What happened to him?) He got shot, I guess he got shot. They're trying to operate on him. (Who shot him?) Somebody, I don't know. This man right here (the character in the front) looks all innocent-like. He hopes that he make it through. He hopes that he make it through. 'Cause it was his fault of him getting shot and he just would of listen to him. He say, he sorry for what happened, it's his fault, "Please forgive me."

Here the older man was pictured by Pete as not protecting the boy from an unknown assailant. Maybe the boy would not have been shot at all if the older man had just listened to him. Now an attempt on his life could even lead to his death, so the boy became the innocent victim of the older man's neglect. This was as close as Pete came to allowing himself to blame his father for his shattered life. In everyday life Pete's anger and hostility were reserved for his stepfather.

STEPFATHER AS BAD FATHER

In contrast with the way he idealized his father, Pete disliked and feared the stepfather who had come into his home and into his life during his middle childhood.

> Me and my stepfather ain't got no type of understanding. We ain't really got no type of understanding, you know. Like, he want me to, you know, like, they, he want me to do the things, like, let me see how to put this. Like, he want me to do what I don't want to do. He want me to, he want me to do what he want me to do. I know I gots to listen to him, but the things he be trying to make me do I can't see myself doing. Like, I do it, like, he be telling me, like, I don't like, on Sundays he be telling me he wants to see me in church every Sunday, right. When he come to my house I better be in church, I better not be home, you know. I didn't like that. I can't go to

church every Sunday, I gotta stay home sometime. A lot of things. He baby my two younger brothers and like whenever I ask him for something he seem like he don't want to give it to me. So, I don't ask him for nothing.

He wanted his stepfather to be more nurturant, but he was afraid to openly admit this to himself and others.

Pete was put through the third degree when he asked his mother or stepfather for money, something to which they never subjected the younger boys.

Every time I ask one of them for money they wanna' they always, their answer to me is, "What you gonna' do with it, what you want it for?" If one of my other brothers ask 'em, they just give it with no hesitation. So, I just don't feel like asking them, going through the hassle.

According to Pete, his stepfather also joined his mother in keeping a tight rein on him, preventing him from leaving the house to be with his friends, playing basketball, and going to parties.

When responding to sentence completion item 30, Pete replied straightforwardly, "If people only knew how much *I dislike my stepfather,*" and to item 35 he said, "People shouldn't *beat their children.*" In response to item 66 he stated, "It hurts when *I get hit with a belt,*" the instrument his stepfather used for beating him.

But, see, like my stepfather, he act like, you know, he act real aggressive, you know. Sometime I be scared of him, so I don't say nothing to him . . . Yeah, I mean, last time he, when I was home, yeah. Yep, he beat me (softly). One time I had a swollen eye, but, you know, I left home for a while, went stayed with my aunt. But I don't know about now. I just ain't got nothing to say to him when I go home. Just keep to myself.

The fact was that Pete was very much afraid of this man, frightened of being physically hurt by him. Even though a good fighter himself, Pete could not defend himself against this powerful man who in addition enjoyed the backing of his mother.

Considering that Pete had frequently suffered beatings at the hands of his stepfather, it was understandable that he could perceive his stepfather as all bad and his natural father as all good. Pete's need to contrast the two men also helped him keep the shining image of his natural father intact. The importance to him of maintaining this idealization was also indicated by Pete's failure to mention any of his own father's deficiencies. At the core of these deficiencies was the fact that his father had not even given him support expected of prisoners' families—to make visits to the penal facility and cheer up the inmate with news and hope for release. One wonders whether Pete unconsciously may have held his father accountable for his situation, because without his father there to protect him, he had been vulnerable to injury by his stepfather and others. An indication of these negative feelings toward his father appeared to be demonstrated in response to sentence completion item 17, "He drew back from the touch of *his father's hand.*"

In Pete we see a young man who longed for the safety and security of a close father-son relationship. But both of his earthly fathers had failed him, and he had no prospects for entering the safe harbor of a relationship with a strong man, a bond which he very much still wanted. Abused and abandoned by these two men who were supposed to be his protectors, he still needed someone to provide him with the guidance he needed for becoming a man. When he was unsuccessful in his search for such a person, he turned to religion. Even though he was made fun of by his fellow inmates for being "saved," he found comfort in taking refuge in Jesus Christ, a man who he believed would not abandon him.

> I, I got saved. I was feelin' so bad, things won't right, I was sad. I, I was cryin', I was cryin' 'cause I felt like I was all by myself. I, I went in the toilet, you know, I closed the door, asked Jesus to, I ask him to take care of me. Then I didn't feel so all by myself.

This was his attempt to find a reliable father and at the same time reduce his sense of loneliness.

Good Mother versus Bad Mother

Pete drew a line across his life separating his experiences before and after the disintegration of his parents' marriage. It was his interpretation that a change came over his mother following this rupture, and that she became the major source of his "family problems." At every interview he brought forth a series of complaints about her, all of which were couched in angry terms.

HUMILIATION

When the need arose for someone to take care of the younger children who were left at home when their mother was at work, Pete's mother gave him the job of looking after his two younger siblings and eventually also the responsibility for doing all the house cleaning and making the meals for the family. It was a heavy burden for a 12 year old to assume, and Pete blamed his mother for the decline in his school work, which he said occurred after she saddled him with these domestic tasks.

My problems started when I was in seventh grade. That's when I started taking all the responsibility like, you know, for the housing, you know, with my two brothers and all of that. I was taking a lot of responsibilities. I use to always bring home a good report card and then I started going down and down. I just didn't care anymore, you know.

The substance of his complaints was not so much about doing the household work and child care, but that he could never satisfy his mother with the way he performed his many duties, no matter how hard he tried. He did not feel that his efforts were appreciated and he never got the nurturance he craved from his mother. He was doing all the caring—with little in return from his family.

My mother, like, she tells me so many things to do and I think I have all of them done, but I leave one out. Then she get all mad, you know, 'cause like I said, "You tell me too many things to do." I just can't, you know, I think, I know all she tell me to do and I do them, you know. I leave one out like she be sending me to the store, you know, telling me to get these couple of things. When I get to the store either I forgot two of them; my mind is already overpacked with too many things. I can't overpack it with some more.

Forgetting was possibly his passive-aggressive way—along with not doing well in school—of telling his mother that he did not want to be tied down at home all the time and treated "like a maid" by her and the rest of the family. One of the most humiliating experiences he had at the hands of his mother was being ordered to cut her toenails.

Made me mad, made me just wanna' snap. How I got ordered around was like, I'm a little, like I was a maid or something, you know. Like, something I never did say, all right, I used to have to do her toenails. She say, "Do my toenails for me and then you can go out." I used to be mad. It usually made me mad . . . 'cause if she asked my brother, 14, he would say, "No, I ain't doing that; I ain't doing your toenails." He'd say it just like that. If I said it just like that she would smack the taste out of my mouth or something like that. But he say that and then she call me to do it, you know. You know, she let him have his way and all that. And that just be making me mad. I got to do that before I go out . . . I did it, but I didn't want to do it. It made me seem like I was a slave . . . she wanted me to cut her toenails then uhm, take up on the little toe if she had a corn she wanted me to take that off. And aah, with a fingernail file to go between her toes.

When his mother asked his brother to perform this degrading task, he refused, but Pete was unable to confront her even though he stated he did not want to be ordered around like a child. When his household work went unappreciated he felt used and insufficiently cherished by his mother. Being treated like a slave and a maid by his mother brought him to the point of hating her, although when he spoke about it he quickly shifted from saying he hated her to the theme of suicide as a means of escaping from such humiliation.

> I don't like to say the words. Sometimes, aah, she makes me hate her sometimes. But I can't say I hate her, but, you know, that's how I feel sometime. I don't feel sometime, I was gonna' kill myself one time, but I couldn't do it . . . You see I was getting tired of, see, like, how she used to nix me when she be on the phone. Like, if one of my other brothers ask her for something, you know, she would just talk right out, you know. She would answer them, but when I go ask her she just look at me like she don't even hear me. So, one time I got mad and just left anyway. 'Cause I was tired calling her, you know, and she wouldn't even look at me. So, I just left the house.

Again, he was ignored, not seen, not cared for. He felt totally rejected in spite of his going against his own wishes and doing what she told him to do. He could not find a way to make her care for him. Was this why he thought of killing himself? "I was fed up and tired. Seem like I could never do nothing right. Seem like when I do do something right, it's wrong. So, I was tired of it."

Pete's hatred of his mother, once expressed, was quickly denied and then replaced by suicidal thoughts. He seemed to turn the hostility he felt toward his mother into aggression against himself. Contemplation of suicide by a lonely person with family problems was described in Pete's response to TAT card 3BM.

> This is not a gun, is it? (Whatever you see it as being.) Well, look like a lady, lady crying. Maybe she had a problem and she look lonely, upset. She looks all upset, worried. Look like, look like a gun on the floor. Guess she say she gonna' solve her problem like that. She look lonely, worried, and all disgusted. Look like she having a nervous breakdown. Crying about something. (What do you think she's crying about?) Guess she got problems. She has something on her mind. Maybe it might be family problems. She just can't take it no more. She want to end it right here. (What will she do to end it? What happens in the end?) Guess she, she gonna' take uhm, she's thinking about taking that gun off the floor and just commit suicide. She look down and out. Maybe that's the way she feel. That will settle it right there. Just because she sad. A lonely lady.

We might speculate that by ascribing a female identity to the person on the stimulus card (actually an ambiguous figure) Pete was projecting on himself that hated feminine role of the maid and slave, a role that allowed him to be humuliated and subjugated by his mother. The nervous breakdown would then represent his response to this unbearable situation and also to the sense of isolation he felt in his family. The resolution was not aggression against those persons causing the family problems but rather self-destruction.

DOMINATION AND INTIMIDATION

Although it was evident that Pete was afraid of his mother, at the same time he wanted to free himself of her domination of him. This was reflected in his story to TAT card 4BM.

> A lady and a man. The lady trying to talk to the man. Seem like he don't want to say nothing to her. He kinda' don't want anything else to do with her. Maybe she did something wrong, something he disliked. She trying to talk to him, but he just turning his head away from her. Like, I guess he just don't hear. She trying to turn him around toward her, but he won't look. He turning his head away from her, like he don't see her. I guess he nonaccept it, I guess he don't want to accept it, anymore. Or, he don't want no part of it. He says, "Let's just end it right here. I don't want to have nothing else to do with you." That's it.

Pete pictured himself as making a feeble attempt at neutralizing his mother's control and domination, but doing it in such a fashion that he did not expose his hostility—"I guess he nonaccept" the relationship. Pete's passivity fed into his subjugation by his mother, for he was always afraid that if he got openly angry with her she would retaliate by hitting him.

> I: Was it okay to get openly angry with your mother, could you do that in the house?
> P: Nah, she would smack me. You can't get angry to her. She would smack me (softly).
> I: She wouldn't go for that at all.
> P: At least I never did, but I know she would smack me.

But it was possible that Pete was concerned with something much more threatening than the pain of his mother hitting him. The larger issue may have been that he was afraid that he might find out that his mother was stronger and possibly more masculine than himself. A male adolescent such as Pete, who has been cast in the roles of maid, slave, and caretaker, might well have been frightened about the possibility that he had adopted and accepted such debasing identities. He never tested his mother to see who would win in a contest between them of power and will. The best he could do was to take the more passive avenue of not wanting "anything else to do with her," which also reflected his sense of despair and feelings of incompetence in dealing with his mother.

In the Draw-A-Person exercise Pete drew a female who had intimidating qualities much like those of his mother (see Fig. 2.) Pictured as having some attractive features (curly hair and soft lips), she was also drawn in a posture that made her appear defiant. Her eyes were piercing, almost cutting right through the observer. The upper portion of her dress resembled a suit of armor more than a woman's garment, and the figure as a whole was sharp and angular, lacking any of the soft curves which might signify femininity. Comparing the female figure with the male Draw-A-Person figure (see Fig. 3, p. 81), the former was significantly taller and more muscular—a stronger and more dominating figure than the attributes of his self-image. Pete had generally portrayed her as a rather fearsome looking individual, not to be tangled with by anyone of either gender, certainly not by an adolescent boy who was both shorter and slighter than she. But because he drew her as having pretty soft-looking hair and lips it may have reflected a different view of his mother, as not all bad. It suggested he would like to have experienced some of her softness and caring that she gave to others, but not to him.

Pete's story in response to TAT card 13B presented the male as thinking about rebelling against his mother's domination and escaping the premises, at least temporarily:

> Poor boy, he looking sad and fed up with this. "You can't do nothing around here, but sit around, just look. I want to go somewhere, go somewhere and have some fun. Get away from here for a while, get around, get from around here for a while. See some new faces. Should I do it or shouldn't I? Should I or shouldn't I? Fuck it, I'm going anyway. I be back before she know it. Go out and have a little fun. Sneak off before she even know I'm gone, I'll be back. I'll be right back." (Who is she?) It's his mother. He'll be back before she even know it. "If I get caught, that's me, that's my, that's my butt. She won't even know it, I'll be back. Be right back."

FIGURE 2.   Pete's First Drawing for the Draw-A–Person Test.

Although Pete has found it difficult, even impossible, to express anger openly toward his mother, the boy in the story defiantly said, "Fuck, I'm going anyway." But, of course, he muttered it to himself, not to her. That he must sneak away to have any fun further demonstrated that he still could not challenge his mother's regimentation directly, but that he wanted to assert himself. He would take the chance of leaving the premises to enjoy himself elsewhere even if he was punished if he got caught, and he had to come back.

In response to the sentence completion items, Pete expressed in many different ways how hard it was for him to contend with his mother. To item 23 he said, "There is hardly any *understanding between me and my mother.*" In response to item 70, he replied, "A mother is more likely than a father to *love the father best and abuse you.*" To item 40 he continued to describe how his mother mistreated him: "The best mothers may forget *she hurts me sometime.*" But it was his response to item 15 that showed he thought his fear of his parents was very unusual—"Few children fear *their parents.*" How would this perception of his mother loving others better than him affect Pete's relation with other females?

INFANTILIZATION

Although it was important for him, as is true for all normal adolescent males, to try to behave in a more adult manner, he felt that his mother wanted to keep him "a little boy." He expressed it in this way: "She treats me too much like a baby, she don't want me to go nowhere."

As Pete grew older and wanted to have activities outside the home, he felt his mother was making deliberate attempts to keep him from growing up and joining his friends. He especially resented being kept from the things teenage males like to do—those activities that constituted steps toward independence from his mother and toward the performance of more manly roles. Pete gave an example of how he felt his mother attempted to stop him from being a man.

I be sitting out on the front porch with my two little brothers. Man, I be so fired up. She make me put on short pants, like I want to put on some other clothes, she said, "put on the short pants, you only going to sit out on the porch." I mean, people, like, friends be coming around to see if I be going here, see if I be going to play basketball. "No man, I can't go, I got to stay on the porch." I be fired up.

The term of reference "little boy" was one that he abhorred, but one he used to describe the boy in TAT card 1. Pete's story about this projective card portrayed the figure as a little boy who was lonely and indecisive.

A little boy sitting down. Looks like a little boy sitting down with something on his mind. Guess he, guess he won't, guess he learn, trying to learn to play this thing. It might, it must be hard to him to learn how to play it. He look lonely, like he got something on his mind. Thinking about something or thinking how he gonna play this, or thinking what he gonna' do. (What happens in the end?) What happens at the end? (Uhuh.) Uhm. Uhm. Well, he look lonely. Got something on his mind or either learn how to play this instrument. Right here, I don't think he can play it. Uhm, how do you want me to end it? (However you want to end it.) He just looks lonely. That's all, he look lonely. (So what happens in the end?) I don't, don't quite understand. (Okay. I asked you to make up a story about what happens in the beginning, right now in the middle, and what happens in the end.) What happens in the end? (Uhuh.) You want me to tell you what happens in the end with the story I'm saying. (Yes.) I, I don't really know. I'm, I'm not really catching on. (Okay. I'll explain it to you again. I asked you to make up a three part story of what happened before this photograph, what happens now during the photograph, and what happens in the end. Is that clear? If not, I can say it another way.) What happens in the end. (Right. How does the story end?) Oh, how does the story end. (Yes.) Ahm. Like he ahm, just look lonely. Or he look miserable. Look miserable and tired.

Not being able to play the violin reflected Pete's view of himself as not being able to exercise control over his own life. Even in telling the story he found it difficult to create a conclusion for it. It seemed as though he was surprised to be asked to state his opinion about something, indicating how little experience he had in planning his own activities and defining what he wanted for himself. His inability to resolve the boy's problem, which was left vague and undefined, mirrored his own sense of being boxed in and unable to figure out how to extricate himself from the unbearable conditions of his life. Like the boy, Pete was isolated and did not know where or to whom to turn for assistance, a tired miserable boy.

Whether knowingly or unknowingly, Pete's mother, from his perspective, had discouraged his attempts to individuate and separate from her and other members of his family. One way he found to express his developing manhood was by having a girl friend. When his mother discovered this, she tried to put an end to it, but Pete refused to bow to her in this matter and continued to see the girl behind his mother's back. The relationship with his girl, Gloria, grew in importance to him, and as time went on his mother finally accepted it. This might have been helped along by the fact that the girl deferred to his mother and would do various chores for her around the house.

For a young man who felt so lonely, unappreciated, and unloved by his mother, being able to express his masculinity and potency by having a girl friend was of enormous importance. In time the two of them became sexually active and Gloria became pregnant when they both were 14 years old. Being a father made him feel proud and important. But his mother reacted in a way that made him feel she was trying to rob him of much of the pride and pleasure of being a father.

> I don't know (softly). I really don't know. Just like, like my girl friend she had a baby, right. So, like my mother, a nurse, and she was telling me like when she didn't think I could of did it, you know, all of this and that. So they didn't want me to see the girl and I guess they didn't want me to see the baby. But I was seeing them anyway, you know.

Pete's mother kept on insisting that Gloria must have been impregnated by an older male, an infantilizing blow to Pete's manhood. In fact, she remained unconvinced that Pete was the father until his older brother, Ray, his favorite sibling, took her to the hospital to see the baby. "My brother tried to tell my mother that he know it was my baby, but when she went to the hospital when he was first born, my brother took her up there and he said he looked just like me, you know."

Pete talked about the birth of his son with a new found sense of a maturing self.

> I: How do you feel about being a father?
> P: I feel happy; I'm proud of myself. And like, I don't know, I know I feel happy and proud of myself. I don't know how my mother and them feel, I know I feel happy.
> I: Is that another way of being a man also by being a father, makes you feel better about yourself?
> P: Yeah, it makes me feel better about myself, like, it don't really make me feel, you know, like, I'm not a man yet, but I'm somewhere around there. But I know I took on some responsibility, but I'm not a man man, but I'm getting there.

The love relationship Pete had with Gloria allowed him to get in touch with a feeling of manhood, and permitted him to escape those images of himself as "a maid" and the "little boy" that continuously plagued him while at home. Pete felt that Gloria was the one person who really understood him and the problems he was having at home; she even encouraged him to try to make the best of the difficult and tense situation within his family. Gloria had engaged another girl with whom he was having a sexual relationship in physical combat over him. That she saw him as worth fighting for made him feel that he was truly worthwhile. As they became more intimate, they were having sex almost daily—a sign, according to Pete, she really loved him and had an exclusive relationship with him. He perceived her as being different from the other girls in his neighborhood, most of whom were sexually promiscuous and smoked marijuana. She even continued going to school after giving birth to their son. The alliance between Pete and Gloria had a degree of permanence, but serious problems stemming from his personal conflicts also plagued the relationship. It was on Gloria that he vented his anger following one episode of particularly infantilizing interaction with his mother:

P: I be burning up on the inside, I be ready to fight. I don't be caring, if somebody even bump into me, I be ready to fight. I just be fired up. One time I even beat up my girl friend. I just don't know why I even beat her up.

I: Do you recall what had happened before that you were so angry you beat her up?

P: Yeah, like, my mother, like, I asked her for some money, you know, 'cause like I wanted to go out. I wanted to go to the movie with these girls, right, but she ain't give me no money, right. So, I only had like about $2 so then I asked if I could go out. She finally let me go out since she ain't want me to go to the movies. So, then I went over there (to Gloria's home) and she just said something and I just went off. I just hit her.

I: Do you remember what she said to you?

P: Something like don't why do you have an attitude, or something like that. I just went off, I just hit her. I just hit her. I didn't mean to hit her.

Because Pete was afraid of expressing anger towards the source of much of his frustration and self-deprecating feelings he physically abused the one who loved him most and who would not attempt to retaliate by withdrawing her love. In light of these new perceptions of himself he was less inclined to live within the old latitudes set up by his mother. When his mother denied him the freedom to participate in the normal adolescent activities outside the house after he had performed all of his various childcare and household maintenance tasks, he grew increasingly angry and frustrated. However, these emotions were discharged not in the direction of his mother, but towards other people and objects.

P: It seem like if I get mad my whole self just change, you know. I just feel like doing anything, anything I can get my hand on, I wanna' hit the person with it.

I: You never did hit your mother though, you never did hit her at all.

P: Nah, I wanted to, I just didn't . . . I just be, I be going out the house, I be going downstairs talking to myself, "I ain't coming back to this motherfucking place no more," you know. I be talking to myself walking down the street because I be so mad.

Pete would usually round up a few older and more experienced boys to help him vent the rage churning within him. He would seek out these more aggressive boys—those he called "the wild ones"—to help him do what he did not think he could do by himself.

P: I go find some of the wild ones, you know, go find one or a couple of them wild dudes who like to go through things like that and being with them. I wouldn't get my best friend to go with me, I just go find them wild ones and just go with them.

I: It seems as though you found something out there with those wild ones you couldn't get anyplace else. What did you find with them?

P: What did I find out, aah. If I go with the wild ones I don't be thinking about my problems. I don't be thinking about my problems.

I: How would you feel then?

P: I guess I be so mad, so burned up I just don't care anymore. I go out there and do anything. That's how I think I be . . . I don't be feeling nothing, I just be high. I just don't be caring. I, I be fired up, I'd be burning up inside and I just don't care. I don't care what happens. I don't care, that's how I be feeling.

When he had broken into a house he would go wild. Excitement replaced loneliness, despair, and burning anger.

Sometimes I just tear it up, just tear it up, you know. Be throwing everything around and knocking this down, doing all that ole' stuff. Jumping, just jumping on the bed and just jump right in the closet, just throw everything out.

Such destructive behavior was the precise opposite of his conduct at home where he was the "maid" who had to keep the entire household in order. These acts of vandalism in other people's houses represented a compensation for his passive compliance with his mother's expectations and wishes. On another occasion he described a different dimension of the feelings he had following a rampage through someone's place.

After you finish doing a B and E, like, you go in a house and you throw everything around and kick a lot of things around, throw this out the closet and throw this off the bed and all that. Yeah, you feel all right after you come out of there. You come out laughing and all that.

Having carried out the promptings of his rage by wreaking havoc on the possessions of strangers, the release came in laughter. He had been able to behave in a reckless, destructive style that was the opposite of the feminine role he had to play at home. In the maid's role he had to clean behind others. By throwing things around and messing up a house he was making others clean up after him. Acting in the role of the tough, masculine destroyer made him feel filled with feelings of power. In this way he broke out of the feminine confinements engineered by his mother and proved his identity as "a real man."

The rage that had become a major feature of Pete's personality and that led him to seeking means for its discharge was also seen in a number of his TAT productions. The anger revealed in these stories was usually directed against women, presumably representing his mother, the one person who he felt had hurt and humiliated him most of all. It should also be recalled that Pete had been arrested for acts of malicious damage of the property of a woman who had thrown water on him. On another occasion he had been arrested for assault on a woman with a butcher's knife. In his stories of acts of aggression with weaker targets Pete expressed his wish to be in a position of power and control over them. His response to TAT card 6BM gave indications of the connection of the two kinds of delinquent acts he committed most frequently: malicious assault on women and breaking and entering.

> A lady check in the room. She might think she hears somebody. Or somebody in there. She look afraid. She look afraid, like somebody's in there. She might be in there by herself. She afraid, she hears noise. Or maybe she hears rats running around, the wind blowing. She comes in the room checking to see if anybody there. She making sure she's the only one in there, nobody else. No burglar. Nobody trying to break in. She's just checking it out. That's it.

Although in the story the crime of burglary was not executed, its possibility did create apprehension and fear in the female figure who was depicted on the stimulus card. Although the story can be read as expressing Pete's own anxiety and insecurity, it may also reflect his need to intimidate women and render them helpless. It is possible that he felt frightening a woman—placing her at an emotional disadvantage (the position that he was frequently forced to adopt by his mother)—was better than a burglary itself. For in this way he could accomplish the desired end of intimidating a woman, but without the risk of actually committing a crime.

During the interviews Pete had stated a number of times that he restrained himself from expressing his anger openly toward his mother on account of the possibility that it might lead him to doing something dreadful, although he never said what such an act might be. His unspoken fear may have been that he might kill his mother if he did not keep himself in check. Although his conscience might not have allowed him to execute such a violent act, the stories to cards 18BM and 18GF both include accounts of women who have died following a fall. The first of these cards showed a man being grabbed from the back by three hands. Pete told this story about the scene:

> The man is saying, "No, let me go, I didn't do it. I didn't kill her. I didn't kill her. It wasn't my fault, she slipped. She hit her head on the table, I didn't do it. Let me go. She slipped and hit her head. I didn't kill her. Please, let me go. She fell and hit her head. It was a mistake, it wasn't my fault. She had it coming."

Here the male appeared to be apprehended by the police for the killing of a female who was not even present in the stimulus picture. The man protested repeatedly that he did not kill the woman in question and explained how it happened accidentally. But no matter how her death had come about he was quick to add his opinion that "she had it coming." In response to card 18GF he produced another story about a woman's accidental death.

> Lady holding another lady in her arm. I guess the lady died. She crying, she said, "Please don't die, you're gonna' be all right. Everything is going to be all right, just hold on. They're coming soon. I don't know what happened. She just, when she was coming down the stairs, she just fell. I don't know what happened. Please help me. Just hold on, everything gonna' be all right. When they get you to the hospital everything is gonna' be all right. Hold on, you'll make it. Okay?"

In this story about two women, the words (attributed by Pete to the woman who held the deceased in her arms) gave expression to some of his own personal struggles, and especially to those connected with his relationship with his mother. If the dead woman is thought of as a projection of his mother, the other figure might be seen as Pete's feminine self, i.e., that part of him that remained attached to her.

Although his masculine active self might have momentarily dared to wish that his mother was dead, his passive weak self could not conceive of committing matricide, an act that would have cut short his mother's domination over him. Instead the whimpering dependent child in him disavowed any role in the serious injury, which had befallen the woman, and he protested repeatedly and too much that it had been an accident. Moreover, although at first he said that the lady was dead, he was quick to assure himself that she was in fact not dead, but only injured, and that help was coming to save her life. The "baby" in Pete—the weak, feminine, and passive part of him that he despised so much— seemed incapable of cutting the bond of infantile dependence on his mother.

Gang as Masculinity Model

According to Pete, the other boys in the gang he belonged to were having personal difficulties with their own families similar to those he was experiencing. They shared their problems with each other of not being understood, appreciated, or wanted by their families.

> P: They be there when you need them. If you really need them, you know. It was like family, all of us were like family. We had like a treasury, you know. We pay our dues and all of that and sometimes when one of us need some money, you don't have no money you just go ask the treasurer if we can take this much, whatever . . . We had an understanding of each other and all of that. Each and every one got attention from each . . . We sit down and talk to each other, and they be talking to me about the problems they be having with they family, you know. I really don't be getting into my problems, but, you know, I say, "Well, me and my stepfather, we don't get along too good," and all that. They say,

"Yeah, man, my father beat up my mother at night," and all that mess. "And me and my brother jump him." They be getting down talking . . . One of them dudes I used I used to meet at his house Friday night, down in his basement. We be getting high and, you know, rapping. It was like a little meeting, we call it a meeting.

I: Okay, so you were getting a lot of your needs satisfied from the group that you couldn't get satisfied at home, the way it sounds.

P: Yep, I know when I get out and, you know, they know I'm out, you know, they going, I know they probably throw a party, like a lawn party, you know, they all right.

Besides serving as surrogate family the gang also provided sanctions for the members' aggressive and antisocial behavior. Although it was important for Pete to associate with the gang for emotional support and physical protection, he did not go along with their ideas of using weapons:

You know, every place we went somebody had something on them, a knife, a gun, whatever. I was kinda' scared, you know, they carrying guns, you know, you know. They let me shoot a gun, you know, I don't like no guns . . . Pull the trigger, "Pow," you know, and it hit something. I just imagine a bullet going inside, inside of me, yeah. I don't like that.

The bigger boys who comprised the gang were also important to Pete because they served as a reference group in furthering the development of his sense of personal identity—but he was afraid of their unbridled aggression. At the same time they helped to give him a greater sense of his masculine self through their fighting and sexual success with females. They were "streetwise" and older than he.

I: So, you prefer being with older people?

P: Yeah.

I: What was it like being with these older guys?

P: Like, I was learning a little bit from them, you know, they be telling, you know, learning streetwise. Learning streetwise, like, like aahm, like ahm, they were telling me that a lot of people out here killing people over, you know, things. I, I was just learning a lot from them, they was putting me, like you learn a lot in the street, they were, like putting me up on a lot of things. Things that I should watch out for and all that.

These male models became internalized images of what he was supposed to be and the way he should present himself to the world outside his home—as a larger and more competent young man, not a little boy. But away from home he still had to face a battle arising from his small stature. It was a cross he had to bear, and one he never seemed to get rid of. Because of his size many people tried to take advantage of him, making it necessary for him to continually prove himself.

Of course, Pete was not the only boy in the neighborhood who was trying to prove himself. Frequently, he found himself having to defend himself against those other boys who wanted to use him as a vehicle to aid in their own perceptions of themselves as "men." Because of his size he was often viewed as easy prey by those boys who needed to dominate others in order to feel better about themselves. Whenever he was referred to as "little boy," he became livid with anger—the term was all the more despicable because it reminded him of how he was treated at home.

Being in a penal facility for delinquent youth placed him in a situation where there were many adolescents who were incarcerated because of their "macho" behavior. Pete described what it was like for him to be surrounded by these bigger fellows:

I just be, I just be wanting to fight sometimes 'cause they uhm, you know, they be, how they coming out on me, you know. They be saying, "Oh, little boy," you know, "I'll hurt you." I had a fight yesterday, a boy mushed me in the face, you know. I didn't hit him then, I told him don't do it any more. He did it again and I went off.

I: What did you do?

P: I beat him up, you know. I hurt my hand, my hand still hurting. I hurt my hand.

I: Because he called you a little boy?

P: Yeah.

I: Did that bother you because he called you a little boy?

P: Yep, and plus he mushed me in the face.

I: So what finally happened?

P: Then we started fighting. He tried to rassle me so I just grabbed him by his neck and was choking him. So, I started punching him, kicking him. The cook . . . he pulled me off.

I: How big was this guy?

P: He was bigger than me. I just don't like, you know, like I told him, to Mr. Hamilton Smothers, I don't bother nobody. He know I don't bother nobody, you know. I told him I wouldn't let him get away with mushing me in the face twice, calling me a little boy. And I told him, "I'll show you what this little boy could do."

I: Uhuh, it sounds like one of the things that really gets you off is for somebody to call you a little boy.

P: Yeah, I don't want nobody to call me little boy.

I: I noticed last week as we were walking across the grounds one of the guys called you midget. How did you feel about hearing that?

P: A lot of people call me midget, you know. They don't really bother me if they call me little man, . . . Godwin, . . .

I: So midget is okay, Godwin is okay, little man is all right, but to be called little boy you don't like that. What's the difference?

P: Little boy, I don't know, little boy, I'm not a little boy, I'm a young man, you know. They call me little boy and I don't like to be called little boy. I guess because my size they say little boy this, little boy that, "Little boy I'll hurt you" and all this and that.

When he was on the streets of Newark he had to face similar encounters, but the stakes were higher because many of his larger adversaries attempted to embarrass him in front of girls. To be embarrassed with females around was a major insult, one that he had to avoid.

P: I just wanted them to respect me, you know, no calling me little boy, you know, trying to embarrass you in front of girls and all that. Saying, "Little boy, I'll hurt you, you can't deal with this," all that. Sometime I just laugh at them, but then they just run it in a hole and I get mad.
I: So, the cats try to embarrass you in front of the girls and that was hard to take.
P: Yeah, if they up there talking to a girl quite sure they don't want nobody to come up to them, "You little boy, you little pussy, you little punk," and all that. "I'll punch you out."
I: How did you want the girls to see you?
P: Not as no little boy, as a young man, as Pete __. That's how I want them to see me. Not as a little boy, I know I'm not a little boy.

Fighting anytime and anybody and committing crimes were ways Pete proved himself to his peer gang where he was the smallest and the other boys were quite large. He also had to show he measured up in his relationships with the girls where it really counted—in bed. Because he was so short, he had a problem with girls who were taller, even though younger than he. When they asked him his age, it was hard for them to believe he was 16 or 17 when he looked like "just a little boy."

Competition was keen among these adolescent males as to who "was getting the most or who was getting over, whatever." The attention from the girls—which Pete claimed he enjoyed—enabled him to gain status among his male friends. Successful sexual exploits and conquests made him feel "that maybe I got something that they don't got." It was very important for him to perceive himself and to be perceived by his "partners" as having something they did not have. That something was the ability to be able to have sex with a girl who made herself available to the other boys he knew. It made Pete feel good to be able to say, "Man, you're crazy. I've already had that. You're late. That's some good stuff, right there . . . That's real. I've got that. They're trying, but they won't get it."

The image Pete wanted to create for the gang members, their girls, and for himself was pictured in his male Draw-A-Person production (Fig. 3).

I: (Pointing to the male figure) Can you describe that person?
P: This person? (Uhuh.) It's a man. Seems like I was trying to draw an image of

FIGURE 3.   Pete's Second Drawing for the Draw-A–Person Test.

me, you know. How I want this. (The moustache?) Yeah. An Afro, I had an Afro until I came up here. They made me cut it off. That's what I was trying to draw, an image of me.

Indeed, the image of him was not of an adolescent boy but of the grown man, virile and sexually attractive. He had the large Afro hair style signifying black pride and power, and a moustache and a beard (Pete had no facial hair and, in fact, could not even shave yet). As can be seen, the figure is wearing a shirt with a V-neck open almost down to his belt, reminiscent of Pete at the time of the first interview when he had left the top buttons of his khaki shirt unfastened. The upper part of the arms looked deformed, but they were drawn this way to widen the shoulders. In the "self-portrait" he compensated for his lacking height by wearing platform shoes, high heels, and an Afro, which comprised a significant portion of his height.

Dreams of Independence

Almost every aspect of Pete's life, even his dreams and aspirations, were tied to disproving his mother's opinion of him that he was a failure.

I wanna', I wanna get settled. I be thinking a lot of things what I wanna' be doing, what I wanna' be doing for the future, you know. I always say, "Don't worry about it, I'm gonna' make it, I'm gonna' make it. I'll be up there on top one day." I'm just gonna' do it. I seems like, you know, my mother don't, seem like, "He's too bad, he can't do nothing." I'm just gonna' prove that I can do something. I know I can make something out of myself. I just gonna' do it. I wanna' have my own family and my own house.

Pete had plans to live away from home when he was paroled from the penal facility, possibly to enlist in the army as his favorite brother, Ray, had done. He stated,

> It will help me out once I get in there and be in there about 3 years. And when I get out I won't have to be depending on nobody and I won't have to be stooping this low and doing this, doing all that for nobody and no asking nobody for nothing. I'll have what I want.
> I: To feel you have to stoop low for your mother and stepfather?
> P: Seem like I was a maid, you know. That's how I felt about the whole thing. Like, I was a maid.
> I: So the army is the way what, to get around some of that?
> P: Yeah, getting around it. Go on my own so I don't have to be bothered. Move far away. That's what I want to do.

Enlisting in the army would be a socially acceptable means of joining the ranks of men who were independent of their families, but he failed to see that his view of the army was unrealistic. His quest for independence and self-validating achievement was reflected in his story in response to TAT card 17BM.

> The man is saying, "I'm gonna' make it to the top. Got to beat him to the top. Got to climb all the way up. I want to be first, the first one that made it to the top. Nobody else but me. I ain't got but so far to go to try to get to the top." So that I can say, "Yeah, I was the first one. I won, out of all the bunch, I was the first one who made it." I could say that to everybody. Trying to get to the top. You want to be the first to the top. So he could tell everybody that he touched the top first. He wants to be known. Known for something.

In these hopes for being recognized for something, even to the extent of beating out the rest of the "bunch," Pete did not rely on Gloria completely to share in his dream. Although entertaining the possibility that he could achieve the American Dream of owning a house and installing Gloria and two children in it, he feared she would not be loyal to him. He described a dream about his future dealing with these issues.

> I was living in my own house, I was married, me and Gloria, that's the dream I had. And aah, every night I say my prayer and I hope that do come true. Everything, you know, I had a little daughter that's all I really wanted two kids, a little daughter and a son . . . If she ain't doing nothing while I'm in here, you know, with nobody else I'm gonna' stay out and make some progress. I'll let her know I can stay out of trouble, make something of myself. I'm going to show them all.

His statement, "If she ain't doing nothing while I'm in here" exposed his doubts and fears about her fidelity and loyalty to him. Would she be a woman like his mother who had a series of men come and go? It did not take much to shake his faith in Gloria. He jumped to unjustifiable conclusions about her intentions without considering her circumstances. After seeing her on a furlough, for instance, he returned looking very depressed.

I: What happened while you were on furlough?

P: A lot of things. I went over there (to Gloria's house) Friday when I got home, you know. She told me her mother had gotten married and they moving down South, you know. They had left Saturday night. I just seen her Friday. I told her maybe we'll meet again.

I: So, you weren't aware of that at all.

P: No, no, not until after I got home.

I: What was that like for you, Pete, to have been told that on Friday?

P: It was hard and I was shaken. Ain't nothing I could do. So, I said, "All right."

I: Was it really all right?

P: Nah, not really. I really didn't want her to leave, but ain't really nothing I could do. She said she be coming back up here sometime in August, sometime up there, you know. I told her, "You probably won't know me then." She's doing what she want to do now.

I: You make it sound as though you're afraid she's going to forget you.

P: I don't really care, you know. Now I don't really care, she's gone now. She ain't nowhere up here. Ain't no telling what she, you know, she don't know what I'm doing whenever I come home.

I: You said you don't really care. I don't believe that. I don't believe you don't really care.

P: I don't, I'm for real. She's gone now. She gone.

I: Okay, she's gone, but I think you really care, though.

P: Oh, yeah, I care about her, yeah.

I: Why do you say you don't care when you really do care?

P: I don't really, I don't really care what she do 'cause, you know, even though I care for her I don't care what she do, you know.

I: I don't believe that either. 'Cause you know why, Gloria has been, next to your brother, Gloria has been the most important thing in your life. Her and the baby. The one thing that has been keeping you going, man, has been her and the baby. And now you tell me you don't care, I think that's bullshit.

P: I don't know.

I: What you are trying to say is that you do care, but you can't tell yourself that you care. Is that it? You're laughing, talk to me. Talk to me.

P: She gone now.

I: I know she's gone, but you do care the way it sounds to me.

P: Oh, yeah, I do care, yeah. I ain't really want her to leave.

I: Okay, that's straight stuff there. What I hear you telling me is that you were hurt to hear that, man.

P: Yeah, I was hurt. I just left, went out and got me something to get high with. Just went to the bar, me and my brother.

I: So you wanted to get high, huh. Seems like you wanted to get away from all of it, huh?

P: I didn't really want to leave, you know, but when she told me it hit me all of a sudden. I didn't really know what to say . . . I was just mad, you know, hit me all of a sudden. It just hit me . . . If I get out, if it's possible I'll try to go down there.

I: See, Pete, you have a hard time telling people things like that, man.

P: I don't know why, that's how I am, I don't know why . . . She really hurt me, I don't want anything like that to happen no more.

I: I think you are being honest with yourself now, you got hurt.

P: Yeah. I don't want to run into this no more. I don't want this to happen no more. You get into a girl and then all of a sudden she's gone. It makes you mad.

I: What did you want to do? You were so mad, what did you want to do that day?

P: I was so mad I probably wanted, I just probably wanted to just take my son and just leave, you know. I just gonna' take him and leave, but I said no . . . I didn't want to take him.

As soon as Gloria told him about her moving south his first thought was to take his son and leave. He actually ended up quitting the scene and getting high. He also entertained the thought of physically hurting Gloria: "I was mad, I was real hurt, and I didn't want to hit her."

I: You were afraid you would hit her?

P: Yeah, so I just left.

I: So, maybe what you really wanted to do was that you were afraid you would give her the hurt she was giving you.

P: Probably, yeah. I know I was hurt, hurt, shocked. I still be thinking about it at night, trying to get it off my mind.

He appeared to be utterly preoccupied with the frightening thoughts of losing Gloria, severely limiting his ability to understand her situation as it appeared to her.

I: Why do you think she had to leave?

P: 'Cause her mother had gotten married, she had gotten remarried.

I: Any other reasons she may have left you?

P: I don't know . . . I know her mother was probably upset too 'cause ah, her daughter, her other daughter, had got killed.

I: Got killed? When?

P: I think it was last month, ah, her sister had got killed . . . she had got shot. She was using those needles (shooting heroin), you know, and she had went out with two dudes who were up here, I forgot their names. All three of them had gotten killed . . . I guess her mother was probably, you know, still upset about that. She just got married, just left.

I: What happened that Gloria's sister got shot? Do you know the details behind it?

P: All pulling, pulling a armed robbery . . . She was on them drugs. I use to tell her, I know Gloria's sister been, I knew her. Me and Gloria's sister use to be, you know, together. I use to tell her to stop using that dope, to cut that out . . . But now, ain't nobody but me now.

When he considered how Gloria could have misinterpreted his behavior, he admitted that "She probably thought I didn't care, you know, by the way I act." But he was already writing her off and saying they had no future together.

P: She might be doing anything . . . Probably, probably already found her a associate now, you know.

I: Associate, what do you mean by associate? Is she in a business of some sort (laughs)?

P: No, she already found her a boyfriend.

I: So, you feel she's with somebody else already.

P: I don't really know.

I: But that's what you've been saying. She left here on Saturday and today is Wednesday and she has somebody else already, huh? You don't trust her, do you?

P: No, not really. But if she come back I'll probably see her. I want to see her, you know. (Softly) I have to see her. I look forward to her coming, but it will be a while. She should be back.

Grudgingly, he conceded to the conflict between his deep desire for Gloria's love and his vulnerability to betrayal by her.

I: You see, I hear two different things at the same time. One thing I'm hearing is well she's down there and maybe involved with somebody else or well, maybe she'll be back sometime soon. Let's come clean for a moment, okay? Do you want to see her?

P: Yeah, I want to see her.

I: But you still don't trust her. Why don't you trust her?

P: I don't. I just can't, I don't know. She probably be going, you know, if she ain't going with nobody else maybe she started going out somewhere. I don't know who she gonna' meet. But I do want to see her again.

I: But it sounds as though you find it hard to admit that to her or yourself that you want to see her again—you want things to go on as they were before.

P: Yeah, I wish they could.

I: But Pete, I think you have a problem saying that to her. She doesn't know where you're at (his feelings toward her).

P: I know. I don't know where she's at at this point. Oh, I ain't afraid to admit that, that I still like her and all that. I ain't afraid to say that.

I: Maybe you're not afraid to admit it to yourself, but maybe you're afraid to admit it to her.

P: No, no I'm not. It just caught me by surprise when she told me (she was leaving). Like, I was in a daze.

I: It might be very important for you to communicate with her.

P: Yeah, I am. I ain't even, I ain't even got as far as the address or nothing. I just left, you know. I have to go over her aunt's house.

I: Do you think you have enough guts to write her?

P: Yeah.

I: I thought maybe you felt so wounded that you couldn't even write to her, maybe.

P: (Smiling) I can write to her.

I: You are smiling, what are you smiling about?

P: I've got enough guts to write her, but she just better write me back.

I: (Laughs) Okay.

P: (Softly) I write her, but she better write me back.

The core of many of Pete's struggles to assert himself was his fear of opening himself to others, even to those persons who had shown they cared for him. Ever so guarded, he defended himself from harm by drawing mental images of others as being untrustworthy and promiscuous. From this defensive posture he could then tell himself that he did not care what others felt about him when in actuality, as in Gloria's case, he loved her very much but was afraid to articulate those feelings to her openly. After many years of feeling that he had to play such games with his more powerful mother to protect his feelings and salvage his self-respect, he had come to believe that he should be on guard with everyone — most particularly with women. But there was another set of feelings, which drew him to them for succorance, thus underscoring his ambivalence toward women.

As time drew closer for him to be paroled Pete began to speak out of a different side of his mouth in reference to becoming independent and on his own. He began to express some doubts concerning his plans for getting a place of his own or enlisting in the army.

I: Did you ever have dreams about being away from your mother, away from her influence over you?"

P: Yeah, like since I was up here, like, I was thinking about not going back home. I was thinking about living on independent living, but I, I just changed my mind.

I: What made you change your mind about that?

P: I, I won't probably be able to make it. I would probably have to stay here longer 'til they find some place for me to go on my own. I don't think I would make it, you know. If I had a job, you know, I think it would be kinda' hard.

Thinking it might be "kinda hard" was a gross understatement of his feelings — actually the prospect of going it alone was very frightening to him.

Two weeks prior to being paroled he went home on furlough to make plans with his mother and family for where and with whom he would live. The option offered by the prison social worker was that if the family could not work out satisfactory arrangements for him to have a place of his own or live with relatives, she would step in and make other arrangements. Finally, it appeared as if Pete had his first real chance to take the steps toward separation and autonomy he said he desired. But when the opportunity presented itself to do so, he literally ran away from consummating any of the possible plans. After his home visit, he failed to return to the detention center where he would have been confronted with a decision about where to go when he was paroled. Being listed as running away put him in the classification of a fugitive and a dependent ward of the state. As a runaway he would be neither free nor independent for long, because once the police caught up with him, they would return him to jail and cancel his parole. Evidently the vacillating child in Pete was still afraid to test his budding manhood against the unknowns involved in fulfilling his dreams of freedom.

OVERVIEW:
PETE'S PSYCHOLOGICAL WORLD

It is important to understand how Pete's delinquent acts were related to his psychological world. (We can infer from his freedom from psychosis that his earliest years were "good enough" (Winnicott, 1971).) Apparently he had experienced a comparatively secure and happy early childhood up until the time his world fell apart when his parents' marriage disintegrated, an event that he described as having come as a complete surprise. After that, his father saw him infrequently and then stopped visiting altogether. Pete was 8 years old at the time of his parents' breakup, which means he received almost no active fathering during his preadolescent and early adolescent years. From the age of 8 on, Pete had been reared by his mother and her boyfriend whom Pete had refused to accept as a substitute for his natural father.

Despite the fact that his father had lost touch with him, Pete described him as being the center of his world. He continued to declare after those many years of separation that his father was the one person who "understood" him, and was someone he wanted to be like. Such identification with a father was inappropriate at age 17, but the notable feature of this identification was its being with a man who was actually unknown to him except in memory and imagination.

According to Greenson (1968), identification with the father is necessary for the boy in the process of "disidentification" with the mother, as the boy attempts to "free himself from early symbiotic fusion with mother" (p. 370). Pete appeared to be entering this stage of psychological development when his father left him. Although he said that his life had been completely changed by the departure of his father, at the same time he did not lay the blame for the shattering of his world on the object of his identification—the father whom he idealized but did not really know. Still, Pete was working on the developmental issues typical for boys of his age. Muus, (1980) stated:

> During preadolescence and early adolescence, the boy directs his aggressive impulses and his castration fears primarily towards his mother and females in general, while actual conflicts with the father reach a low point. As a defensive reaction against castration fear, the boy shows an exaggerated idealization and aggrandizement of his father. During this negative passive Oedipal phase of early puberty, it is the castrating mother, rather than the father, who is feared and avoided. (p. 244)

Pete fitted this portrait of the inner life of the boy going through the early stages of puberty. The interaction between him and his mother took on the qualities of a vicious circle, a not uncommon phenomenon: the more she restricted him, the greater his need to unloose the maternal fetters. The more he disobeyed her and ran wild with the gang, the more she redoubled her attempts to keep him under her watchful eye. As he saw it, his mother wanted to keep him "jammed up" in the house for no good reason and treated him like "a little boy" and "a maid."

While Pete was full of verbal protestations about being restricted and infantilized by his mother, at the same time a part of him was willing to be defined and dominated by her in this way. There was an ambivalent struggle going on for the possession of his soul. It seemed as though one part of him wanted to please his mother so badly that he tried in every way to play the role of the fastidious housekeeper and the responsible nursemaid to win her begrudging approval. Another part of him, his emerging masculine self, was attempting to become more self-assertive, to be as rough, tough, and mean as a man should be. This ambivalence of Pete's may partly explain why he had to go to such extremes to assert his masculinity. In addition, he may also have resorted to behaving in such a dramatic fashion because there was no father actually available in his daily life after whom he could pattern his behavior in a realistic way.

In addition to his anger at being treated like a kid or a woman, and his difficulties with shedding these roles, Pete had enormous concerns about being so short. His preoccupation with size was a constant in his reactions to other people, making him hypersensitive to slights, both real and unintended, and quick to defend his honor and manhood by fighting. His excessive bragging about the fights he had won and the girls he had "made" may be explained partly by the heavy emotional burden his small feminine build placed on him. His shortness added another dimension to the worries about somatic development typical of most adolescents. About these preoccupations, Muus (1980) wrote:

Boys especially are disturbed and troubled by such deviation from the normal course of development, even though most of these fall within the normal range and are temporary. Such physical deviations negatively influence the individual's social and emotional responsiveness, as well as general attitude toward life. As a defense during this phase, an exaggerated preoccupation with maleness and masculinity in the boy emerges. (p. 246)

Pete's acts of violence could be looked at as his way of recapturing and reasserting a sense of power and masculinity and to ward off feelings of feminine weakness. These antisocial acts were generally of three types: attacks on women, breaking and entering, and gang fighting. All three of these were methods by which he was able to establish what was not validated about him at home—that he was a man. Concerning his assaults on women, including his girl friend, he explained, "It seem like, if I get mad, my whole self just change, you know. I just feel like doing anything, anything I can get my hands on. I wanna hit the person." What he appeared to be doing was compensating for the weak, devalued, feminine, and passive self, contained in the role of being a "maid" who was the "slave" of his mother, by becoming the aggressive active self who broke the rules and felt good about being male.

The many B and E's he pulled also served as a means to express his masculinity. While at home he had to behave in the feminized servile role of a maid, with responsibility for the care of his two younger brothers, cleaning the house, and preparing the meals. His role at home was to keep the entire establishment orderly. But when he executed the B and E's he was in touch with his more masculine, destructive self (Winnicott, 1971). It made him feel "happy"—he was "feeling good" when he was destroying someone else's home, possessing momentarily a sense of power that he had never known in his maid's role. This sort of expressive vandalism was consistent with the "rapaciousness, smuttiness, oblivion to unkemptness, dirtiness and body odor, motoric restlessness, and experimentation in every direction of action and sensation", which aid the adolescent to move further beyond the mother and her controls over him (Blos, 1979, p. 197).

The street gang Pete belonged to and with whom he committed much of his wild and delinquent behavior enabled him to express his own potency fully and to indulge in destructive acts with virtually no inhibitions. The gang also allowed him to place some distance between his mother and himself and the neat and orderly life for which she stood. Writing about the functions of the peer group for youths, Muus (1980) suggested:

The adolescent individuation process contributes to the establishment of a personal, social and sexual identity. It requires turning away from parents and, because of still insufficient autonomy, a temporary turning toward the peer group culture. The latter serves several function for example with the Oedipal conflict during this period, and the need to sever parental dependencies. The peer group may actually serve some functions better than the family. (p. 233)

From the gang Pete learned that it was okay for him to take off his maid's apron and put on the long pants and ways of men.

It is the argument here that Pete's desire to be free from his mother's control was grounded in a genuine developmental need to establish his own autonomy. The appropriateness of what he was trying to do was specified by Blos (1970) as "the shedding of family dependencies, and the loosening of infantile object ties in order to become a member of the adult world" (p. 142). Unfortunately, neither Pete nor his mother (nor those so-called helping agencies) fully understood what his delinquent behavior meant. Many of his acts of delinquency— though socially unacceptable—were pathological expressions of the blocking of his need to move away from infantile dependency into the larger world.

Pete's cries to try "independent living" when he left prison and his wish to join the army were also indicators of his desire to separate and individuate from his mother. But when the first real opportunity arose for Pete to be free and independent, he could not take advantage of it. Instead he ran from the adult responsibility, which he claimed he had wanted for so many years. Faced with the familiar adolescent conflict between the "desire to go ahead" and the "fear of losing familiar ground" (Blos, 1970), Pete sought escape from growing up: Two weeks before his pending parole, when he would have been presented a chance for "independent living," Pete ran away from the penal facility. The prospect of full personal freedom evidently was unbearable, so he chose to remain a ward of the state as a fugitive.

4

The Case
of Sly

There are some delinquent youngsters who have an insatiable hunger for approval. They go to great lengths to win the applause of others no matter how much trouble it causes them. In fact, much of their behavior, both delinquent and nondelinquent, is expressive of a driving need to be affirmed by others. Unable to bear situations in which they are not the object of admiration, they become vulnerable to feelings of emptiness and worthlessness. Sly's delinquent behavior stems from this form of psychological deprivation.

SLY: HIS SELF–PRESENTATION

Sly was a 17-year-old whose boyish face and slight build made him appear younger than his age. Initially he spoke in a halting, unsure manner, but very soon warmed up to having a willing audience and being tape recorded. He was an animated storyteller who took obvious delight in his ability to engage a listener. Much more open than many of the other incarcerated boys who had been interviewed, he spoke at great length about his delinquent and personal history without much prompting by the interviewer.

Sly's Personal History

Sly was the second youngest child in a family of six children. He had three sisters and two brothers. Besides Sly, only his 16-year-old sister and 18-year-old brother still lived at home. He described this sister as his favorite: "She don't try to down me." By contrast, the brother still at home was the one with whom he had the most difficulty: "He tried to take my father's place, you know. I use to tell him, I'm 17, I don't need you to go around all bossy, telling me to do this, to do that, you know." The eldest of the brothers was serving a life sentence for murder at a maximum security state prison.

It was not easy to get a clear understanding of Sly's mother's life from his descriptions of her. From what he said, it appeared that she had six children by the same number of men. Still Sly presented her as a solid maternal figure who wanted the best for her children. In regard to himself he saw her as always trying to get him to behave. On more than one occasion upon suspecting that he had committed a crime, she called the police. At those times he asked himself "Why would she call the cops on her own son?" After some reflection he would conclude, "Look how much trouble I'm been and she be trying to help me." Even though he realized that his mother would "be hurt" when he got into trouble again, it did not stop him. When he was angry with his mother he would generally say, "Fuck it," and "pull another B and E." So he felt that his mother's description of him, "He ain't no good," typified the way she felt about him.

His parents, according to Sly, had been divorced for a long time, and Sly had only sporadic contact with his father for most of his life. Within the last few years even that amount of contact was cut short by the conflict between his parents that culminated in his father stabbing his mother in the back with a butcher's knife. After that his mother told all of the children that she did not want them to have anything to do with her former husband. When his father asked Sly to live with him, he thought he had to refuse because of what his mother had said. Meanwhile, his mother's boyfriend, who had been living as a member of the family for 5 years, tried to take the role of the children's father. Sly said he did not mind the man living within the household so long as he "did not tell me anything or act as he was my father."

When he was 8 years old, Sly was arrested for throwing a cherry bomb, a large firecracker, that demolished a store window. At the age of 14, he began getting into more serious trouble after the family moved from one section of the shore community to a "bad" part of town. Soon a member of a street gang introduced himself and the smoking of marijuana to Sly, and it was not long before he joined his new friend's gang. Influenced by the gang's negative attitudes toward school and his own intense dislike for a teacher at his new school, he discontinued attending class. From then on he began to engage in delinquent acts of an increasingly serious nature, ranging from purse snatching and stealing mopeds to breaking and entering and automobile theft. Sly had been arrested numerous times. He clearly enjoyed telling the story of his parole appearance in juvenile court when the judge reminded him of how many charges against him were in the record and called him a nuisance against society.

It was one of his less serious offenses—a purse snatching—that led to his first stint at the penal facility.

See that, 'cause like I was working and got fired and was pissed off about that, you know. My mother's boyfriend getting on my case, you know, he and my brother and I got pissed off all about that. So, I just went out and done something stupid.

Similar confrontations with his family seemed to trigger many such incidents. His pattern was generally to "get mad and walk out. "I gotta' do things on my own, I didn't like them telling me I can't do this, I can't do that." When he wanted something, he explained, he wanted it "right there and then . . . that's another reason I started stealing. I wanted things my own way, you know."

SLY'S INNER WORLD

Sly had a tendency to present himself to others as if everything was all right, even though he was spending his second term at a penal facility for adolescents. But when pressed and challenged about what he said about himself and his world, it appeared that he was hiding behind a facade of jauntiness and verbosity. An analysis of his statements during the interviews and his projective test protocols assist in uncovering Sly's psychodynamics.

The Female Audience

Sly had many difficulties in his life many of which had to do with his mother and other females. It might be said that females were a source of some of his deviant behavior, because he had such a driving need to be recognized by them.

THE MOTHER

Although there has been difficulty and conflict between Sly and his mother over the years, he realized how distraught she became when she saw him and his other brother behind bars.

> She tried to help all of us the best she could. She'll even, she'll cry, you know, just tell us, that starts making me feel bad. That's why, like, when I was out I was trying to do something . . . It makes me feel bad, you know, to see my mother come visit me while I'm locked up. I mean, you know . . . I know what she's been through.
> I: What has your mother been through?
> S: I mean toward my older brother (the one who is in prison for murder), you know, it's pain, agony. The same thing, "Your son got locked up, you son got," you know, it builds, builds, builds, builds, builds. They (his family) even called the cops on me because I got in trouble.

Although Sly stated that he hated to hurt his mother and add to her agony by being her second son in prison, he refused to listen to her pleas to change his behavior. Though she told him repeatedly that his gang friends were a bad influence, he never took her warnings seriously. In fact, it made him angry with her when she ordered him not to hang around with the boys who had involved him in serious crimes. Referring to one boy in particular, his mother said, "I don't want you around him, you got in trouble . . . If I see you with him I'll call the cops, get you sent back in." At her wits end, his mother would resort to yelling at him and cursing him.

> When she would curse at me, I'd say, "Damn, man," you know, I'd be mad, you know. I say, "Let me leave, get out of here." Then my friends come, say, "Let's do this." I just say, "Fuck it," 'cause I'm mad already. I do this to get that off my mind."

When his mother was upset enough about Sly's bad behavior, she would do much more than curse him. As Sly put it she would lose control and "blow her lid."

> I: What would happen if she lost control?
> S: Start hitting me, start throwing, you know, hitting with chairs, not throwing chairs, just hitting me . . . Like sometime she would say, "Just do that shit, if you don't do it, I'll beat your ass . . . if you don't do those dishes I'll beat your ass," you know . . . I didn't want her to get, you know, to the point she destroy the house . . . Sometime she get a pie and throw it . . . When she gets mad, she just blows her lid.

To escape from her he would usually "leave home and get high. Just go out, go to a party and get blasted, you know, get blind, get all the things off my mind," and sometimes "pull a B and E or something like that."

Sly knew the source of his mother's anger that she could barely control when he refused to obey her—she was desperately afraid that Sly was heading in the direction of serious criminal involvement similar to her eldest son's. Even though Sly appreciated her concern, he still could not bring himself to correct his behavior and not be a problem. His reaction typically was to get mad at her in return.

> I: You were talking about the idea of getting angry with her. You would ask your mother for something and she wouldn't give it to you? Did that happen quite often that you would want things from her and she would not give them to you?
> S: Yeah, it happened, you know, off and on, like. I would ask, you know, everyday for something, like, only, only when I really needed something, say I really needed a pair of sneakers or something. I'd ask her for it and she would say,

"No," you know. I be looking at my side, I don't be looking at, you know, she don't have the money or nothing like that.

I: So, the only thing you'd be thinking of was that you didn't get what you wanted from her.

S: Yeah.

I: And what would you do then?

S: (Laughs) Go out, steal, you know, do a B and E, get some money, probably go buy something. Oh, you know, get what I want.

Repeatedly acknowledging that his mother did not have the money and therefore could not possibly supply him with what he wanted, he persisted in asking her for what he knew she would refuse him. A common reaction to being turned down by her was to break into a home, knock things over, and steal what he could. Afterwards he claimed he experienced a sense of relief. There was a regular association between his anger over being denied by his mother and the satisfaction derived from securing what he wanted by stealing it.

Sly wanted his mother to satisfy every one of his material and emotional needs, regardless of his knowledge of her inability to do so. The idea promoted by his mother that one gains what one wants through work and effort was not something he accepted, no matter how often his mother and others pointed it out to him.

I: You make it sound as though you wanted something from her you never got. What was that?

S: That was love.

I: You thought she didn't love you?

S: We didn't have no understanding between each other, that's why.

A refusal or delay by his mother in granting his request for something was not seen in a practical context of whether she could realistically fulfill it. Instead, when she did not respond to him in the way he desired, he interpreted this as her not loving him. "Love" meant to him being given what he wanted. He regarded the relationship in black-or-white terms: either she gave him what he wanted when he commanded it or she didn't—there was no toleration for frustration of his demands.

Sly drew a vivid picture of his childish role in which he cast himself when he begged from his mother. At the same time he conveyed his sense of resentment over not being treated indulgently when he was small. It was as if he realized that his weaning had been harsh—that he had to cry for a lollipop, the equivalent of the money and clothes for which he continued to ask his mother. Although Sly tried to dispel the impression that he still cried "like a kid" for what he wanted, he depicted himself as fighting constant temptation to badger his mother for what he wanted.

OTHER MATERNAL FIGURES

Although Sly was not fully aware of his need to be the center of attention, he did know that several of his female teachers in elementary and junior high school had made him feel "small and stupid." His response to their giving him "easy work", which made him feel inferior and deficient, was to be truant from school periodically, and he eventually wound up not attending school at all. Similar difficulties occurred with his teacher, Mrs. Copper, at the juvenile penal facility. Within the confined situation where he could not avoid going to class, he had another woman whom he could experience as failing to meet his special needs. In the interview Sly complained repeatedly about how Mrs. Copper treated him:

> It's so much confusion, you got to go through this much work, this school, then hear her smart remarks and when you say something hurt to her she's ready to write you up. You try to talk to her like a man she think you're talking to her like a kid. I told her I wanted to get switched; "No, you can't get switched," (mimicking her). I even told her, I said, "Look like you and me can't get along," 'cause, you know, like, like, I mean, she look at things her only way. She don't want to look at things anybody else's way.

> I: She treats you like a kid?
> S: Yeah, 'cause, yeah. 'Cause this is Glenville she might look at Glenville, yeah they young they still don't know that much. That's how I look at it. She don't want nobody to say something back to her. When somebody say something back to her it must hurt her 'cause she cops an attitude. She hollers at us . . . I tried to tell her . . . I told her today, "If you want respect, you should give us respect," you know . . . She'll holler at us and like, she even cuss. She said, "I won't let any of you MF's take my job."

From his description of the technique employed by Mrs. Copper to establish and maintain control in her classroom it sounded as though he was not getting the preferential treatment he craved. When Mrs. Copper started cursing him out it made him so angry he would come close to losing control:

> Like I want to slam her, I will tell the truth, but I won't hit her, you know. When you try to talk to her peaceably, you know, she seem like she don't want to hear it. She just want to hear what she want to hear. She'll just pick at things, "Why you cursing?" or something like that. She'll just pick out the things she wants to hear.

He needed and wanted someone to really "hear" him, i.e., fully and deeply understand his experience and he reacted to anything less than such total empathy with extreme anger. Referring to Mrs. Copper, Sly said, "I'm trying to deal with it, the best that I can 'cause like, my parole date, I can go home June 9th. I'm trying to deal with it, (softly) but I can't take too much." It was hard for

Sly to accept the classroom structure where he was just one of the many students and he seemed to be acting up to draw attention to himself even if it meant being reproved.

Recalling an instance in which Mrs. Copper had written up a disciplinary report on him, he could not even say her name. In jail it was "this hell" because he had little if any room to maneuver. When he was at home at least he had the street gang as a means of getting attention, but at the penal facility he was locked into a subordinate position relative to the teacher.

During one interview Sly considered the possibility of trying to make peace with Mrs. Copper as a way of ending a war in which he was always the loser:

I: Have you tried talking to her about what is going on?

S: I ask her, you know, I can't even talk to her, man, 'cause it seem like she just want to look at it, you know, her way. She don't want your way.

I: Well, I wonder if you can ask her to talk with her privately about what you feel your concerns are? Is that possible?

S: We talk once.

I: Do you think that could happen again?

S: Yeah, I can try. She be trying sometime.

I: Seems as though you're caught in the middle and you don't know where to turn.

S: They ain't doing their job . . . Mrs. Copper treats me like I'm a dog and she can run over me. I ain't gonna' let her do that . . . then you try to tell her she think you fucking, you know, excuse my language.

I: What were you going to say?

S: Fucking with her, playing games and stuff with her.

It seemed as though Sly could not tolerate anyone not seeing it "his way," showing the narcissistic need for the teacher to be his "selfobject" (Kohut, 1977), i.e., to stabilize and consolidate *his* sense of selfhood.

Three weeks later at the end of an interview Sly mentioned that his relationship with Mrs. Copper had begun to improve following a private talk with her.

Me and Mrs. Copper cool now (laughs). She, she a trip . . . (laughs) you know we kid around, like before everything I did she was all in my shit. But now, you know, I sit by her desk, I be doing my work, she be helping me out. She's all right now.

As was his usual stance with women, Sly could only feel at ease with them if they enjoyed the relationship, "had" a trip, kidded around with him, and gave him special attention like having him sit by her desk. Under those conditions he would do his work and even admit he needed some help. Narcissistic nurturance was being provided by making him feel special and unique, thus enabling him to feel he had a positive self.

But the special relationship between him and Mrs. Copper did not last very long. As he entered the room at the beginning of the next interview it was quite apparent that he was disturbed about something. It turned out he had been denied permission for a special visit home. Although it was an administrative foul-up, Sly chose to blame Mrs. Copper for what he had unjustly been denied.

Having witnessed the disintegration of his special role with Mrs. Copper and lacking the incentive of a home furlough to make him behave, Sly began to act out in Mrs. Copper's class again. He readily admitted that he was "messing up in her class." Because Sly was falling back into the old pattern of making problems for himself as a result of feeling slighted, the interview was turned again to looking at his self-destructive behavior:

> I: Sly, you got to understand about your own behavior also don't you think? You can get angry with her all you want to, what does that wind up doing for you?
>
> S: You can't, you can't, you know, I'm in the position where I shouldn't be doing that, but I just can't help it, you know. When somebody do something and then they laugh, look like they laughing, I get pissed off and just go off. I see sometime when she write me up, she have a smile on her face like she just did it to be funny or something . . . and see, I just, she just like to see people suffer, that's the way I look at it.

Although Sly had a tremendous need to have people laugh with him, here he found himself being vulnerable to being laughed at by his teacher. In this situation he was literally unable to shine as he so desperately needed to do. Sly expressed the rage he felt when he found himself not being the positive center of attention:

> If, if I keep it in, you know, if I keep it in it gonna' build up and build up 'til one time I just gonna', you know, blow my cool . . . and go off. Curse her out, do everything . . . But now I glad I'm out of her class. Now finally I got a chance to prove to her that I won't be in no more trouble.

Even after complaining about how difficult Mrs. Copper was and how angry she made him by not treating him as though he was special, he had the need to "prove to her" that he was really worth paying attention to.

SLY'S GIRL FRIENDS

Although Sly found it very difficult to gain the attention and personal leverage he desired with his mother and female teachers, he thought he was more successful at this with females closer to his own age. He spelled out what he liked about one girl he had gone with for several months before being incarcerated for the second time. He made a commitment to Nancy that he would stay out of trouble, a promise he never made to any girl before.

> I: What was there about Nancy you enjoyed so much?
> S: She give me respect and I give her respect. Like, she, like, some girls, like, you know, she wasn't the kind of girl that will see you one day and be funny the next day . . . the next day you see them seem like they don't even want to know you or nothing. You say, "Hi," they say, "I don't know you," you know. Seem like they don't hear me. She never did that to me.

The idea of being continually recognized and not being snubbed by girls was of paramount importance to him. In addition, he always had a concern about saving face with them:

> Yeah, like the girl I was going with while I was out there, she wanted to go to the movie to see "The Fish That Saved Pittsburgh." So, we went on a Friday . . . I told her I'd be over to pick her up. So, I didn't have any money (laughs), you know, she asked me but I didn't want to, you know, tell her, "No." 'Cause she'd say, "Damn, you're going with him and he ain't even gonna' take you out to the movies." Then I say, "Yeah, I take you, I'll take you to the movie."

Sly did not have the money to get them into the show so he had to ask his friend to slip him the money to cover their tickets.

> "He gave me 10 dollars, you know . . . he slipped it to me, so, you know, don't let Nancy see it. Like, that'll make, you know, I'm pissed off he paying his way and I ain't even paying."

He could not risk taking the chance of Nancy seeing him as he really was—without money. Asked why he did not want Nancy to see him get the money from his friend, Ronald, Sly explained that he could not allow her to see that he was not up to the image of the complete person that he wanted to project to Nancy. He could not risk her seeing behind his mask of the person in control.

Sly also wanted to be seen as physically attractive by girls other than the one he was going with. He described one young woman who knew that he was dating Nancy as being "crazy about me." Although it was acceptable for him to attempt to have sex with other girls, the reverse would not be tolerated on Nancy's part.

> I get jealous, but she'll say, she ask me, "Why can't, why can't I talk, why can't I talk to a dude when you can talk to a girl?" I said, "Put it this way, 'cause you're a girl and I'm a boy, that's you know, you know, that's how boys you know, that's how they gonna' look at it. 'Cause hey, girl," you know.

It can be seen from Sly's description that his ability to identify with his girl friend's point of view was profoundly limited; one gathers the impression that he saw things only from his own perspective and that other people existed for him primarily as objects functioning to build his self-esteem.

Several weeks after Sly told the interviewer that he had proposed to Nancy that they get engaged, he let it slip out that Nancy had not been in touch with him since he had been sent to prison a second time. However, if Sly was angry about this, he did not display it. Evidently it was unbearable for him to face the idea that Nancy might not have regarded him so highly as he had supposed. Instead he began talking about the attention he had been given by another girl friend named Pat:

> I was going with this white girl (laughs), Pat. I was talking to her, you know. She, me, but I didn't like, I liked her, but I didn't like her that much, you know, to be close, you know, with her. She wasn't young, you know, that's that's maturewise. She was about 25. She ask me if I wanna' come home. Usually when you first meet a girl they'll say, you know, "Wait a while 'til you come over, so we get socializing," you know. This girl, you know, wanted me to move in with her, all that stuff. I didn't just wanted the pussy. That's the reason I wanted to go over there and plus, really, to see if she really liked me. If a girl, if a girl ain't really, don't like you she ain't gonna' let you just come over their house like that.

Even though Pat did not appeal to Sly very much—he disapproved of what he called her "wild ways," evidently he was drawn to her by the attention she paid him. Her inviting him to come to her house overcame his reluctance to become involved with her. In fact, he was so caught up in wanting to appear "special" in her eyes that he lied to her rather than turning down her request for some money.

> Uhm, like I told you before, you know, when a girl ask me for something I don't want to tell them, "No," I just tell them, "Yes," not to hurt their feelings. So, she ask me you know, "I need 'bout," you know, "20, 30 dollars," you know, "so we can go out, movie, get some food for the house and stuff." So she ask me do I got it, right. I said, "Yeah," right. I said, "Damn, I should have told her no," you know, "now she gonna' be looking for it." So, I said, "Damn, how am I going to get the money?" I ain't gonna' ask my mother 'cause she gonna' ask me what I want it for and I ain't gonna' ask her I want it for this 'cause she gonna' say, "Nah, you don't need it for that." . . . So, then, you know, that why I snatched that pocketbook, 'cause of her. I got sent back up here for that.

Even though Pat had not been in touch with him since he was incarcerated for an act supposedly committed on her behalf, Sly was giving consideration to living with her after being paroled. But considering the nature of this relationship with Pat, and its short history, Sly was basing his future on sinking sand—on a relationship that had little to support it other than its sexual aspect. Here again Sly was looking to someone else rather than within himself to create some meaning and structure in his life.

For Sly, it was critically important to have a Nancy or a Pat act as though she regarded him as a provider "who had it altogether." Although he tried to perpetuate this desired image of himself, in others' eyes and for himself, he found it was not working with his two girl friends. In addition to the fact that Nancy and Pat had not written while he was in jail, he got a lukewarm and spotty reception from Nancy during his 12-hour visit home. Nancy was civil, but she informed Sly she could not go out with him any longer because of his record and his incarceration for the second time. When he tried to locate Pat, he was informed that she had moved without a forwarding address.

Although Sly vowed that he would not behave in the same way on being paroled one had to question whether he could give up his desire to play the role of the star with his girl friends. Sly had embarked on a life of crime as one of the means he used to gain the affection of women. We know that it was of utmost importance for Sly not to "hurt feelings" of women because he could not bear the possibility of a negative response from them. He may have seen himself as the benevolent protector of women and small children: "Now I won't go out . . . and do something . . . show them that I'm man enough (softly), they don't, you know, have to work." It was as though Sly was struggling to find the best way of securing a special relationship with his girl friends.

Sly was evidently afraid of being seen as a nobody by the girls. He had so little self-confidence that he felt he had to comply with a request for money when he did not have any. That had gotten him involved in "stealing stuff, petty shit, for 50 dollars, stealing it for girls." He could only be sure that they were good friends when he gave them money. It is apparent that Sly, having little or no respect for himself, was seeking in the admiration of his girl friends to find a sense of his own significance and self-worth.

The Male Audience

Sly had suffered the experience of not ever knowing his father in a meaningful way. Much of his self-destructive behavior was geared towards replacing this missing object as a means of feeling more whole as a person.

THE FATHER

As quick as Sly was to make negative statements about his mother, he was equally fast at describing his father in a positive light. Because he hardly knew his father, he was defining how he thought a good father would behave. In his imagination he conjured up a picture of living in an intact family in which his father would have kept him firmly on the right path. The role of a father in the disciplining of a son was critical in keeping a boy from "messing up."

> S: 'Cause I didn't have no one to get on me, my father like. I look at my mother, you know, trying to pity me like, like a little kid. And I never lived with my father and I know father, 'cause he told me if I be messing up he gonna', you know, beat my ass, you know, and stuff like that. It probably 'cause I couldn't get along with my mother at that time. I didn't have no other source to go to, like my father and her was divorced and I couldn't live with my father, so I stayed with my mother. And that's probably why.
> I: So, it was hard.
> S: It was hard living with my mother 'cause I couldn't get along with her and I wouldn't listen to what she, you know, say, And I didn't have nobody else to go to like my father, you know. They were divorced and living else, and I know my mother wouldn't let me go live with him. So, I started fucking up.

It was evident that Sly understood, albeit in his own adolescent way, what the deprivation of not having a father had meant in his life. Just to be told that his "ass" would be beaten if he messed up would have helped. But Sly also knew that he needed more fathering than just those threats of punishment—he was also crying out for a father to understand him and give him that sense of importance he did not get from his mother. Sly felt that if he had at least a "good enough" father he would not have taken the path of delinquency.

Knowing Sly's needs for an idealized father figure, it was not surprising that he went to considerable lengths to keep the image of his actual father unblemished. Even though his father had rarely come to see him since the divorce, Sly would make excuses for this neglect, usually finding a way to shift the blame for his father's behavior to someone else or some special set of circumstances. Explaining why his father had not visited him at the penal facility as promised, Sly minimized his own disappointment by putting up a front of being unflappable when it came to his dealings with his father.

> He said he wasn't sure he could make it 'cause, you know, he didn't have no money, you know. He had some money, but he needed some gas for his car. So, that's why I wasn't really expecting him, you know. I just said, "Forget it." He just didn't get the money, I'll just call him to see if he'll come up next week . . . if he has money for gas.

It was Sly, not his father, who made the effort to keep up the contact between them, and the communication all went one way—from him to his father. In fact, interaction between father and son was virtually nonexistent. Sly did not know what his father was doing, his address, or current telephone number, a fact he discovered when he tried calling his father from the training school. Although

Sly was eventually able to reach his father by tracking down his correct number, his father did not even bother to tell him he was not going to show up for the tentative appointment to visit him in jail.

I: It sounds as though you are able to take disappointment easier from a man than from a woman.

S: I see, I look at it, I look like a man, you know, is coming from, you know, he ain't trying to be funny or nothing, you know, talking man to man. But then when it come from a lady I think she trying to be funny or something . . . It seem like a lady, you know, if they see a man trying to be serious they take it for a joke.

It was clear that Sly needed to keep a positive image of his father intact. Indeed he had pledged a kind of allegiance to his father—"man to man"—that he felt he had to uphold in order to believe that his father really cared for him. Moreover, he was able to deflect the blame for the pain he had suffered to women who "if they see a man trying to be serious they take it for a joke." However, there were growing indications of disaffection in Sly's feelings toward his father. On another occasion when his father broke a promise to visit him at the penal facility, Sly said:

You know, I ain't worried, it ain't on my mind, you know, I ain't even really worried 'bout it. But I don't like people lie to me, that's it, tell me they gonna' do something and don't do it. My sister say, "Why don't you write, why don't you write?" I say, "Why should I, should I write him if he ain't gonna' do nothing for me?"

Finally confronting the true nature of his father's relationship to him—"he ain't gonna' do nothing for me,"—Sly for the first time acknowledged that his father had failed him time after time, occasion after occasion. Although a most uncomfortable and painful realization to encounter, in doing so Sly was free to display the angry feelings toward his father that he wished to avoid. Sly's controlled anger and his need for a better father-son relationship were expressed in his story to TAT card 7BM:

This one, in the beginning, I guess (yawns), it could be, I guess he trying, his father trying to, aah, to talk to him about something. In the middle, he still mad about what happened. (Who is mad?) He is. (The younger man is mad?) Yeah, right here. (Uhuh.) At the end, I guess, at the end I guess he probably talk, you know, talk to him. (Talk to?) Talk to him. (The older man?) Yeah, talk to him 'bout what happened.

It is worthwhile remarking that in this story the direction of communication—from father to son—is the reverse of what was the case in Sly's actual situation. Even though Sly was still resentful he desperately wished that his father would finally provide him the needed attention and talk to him—explain to him "'bout what happened" all those many years that he had not been present and available.

THE GANG

Sly had joined a street gang when the family moved to a new section of town, despite his mother's warnings about the gang members' bad reputations and police records. But Sly was not deterred by the possibility that the gang would get him into trouble because he felt so much better about himself in their company. "They gave me more, you know, attention than they would (his family), you know. It seemed like they would care more for me than would my, you know, they would." At home he felt "hemmed up" and "lost"; in the street with the gang he was "cool"—and felt good about himself. He described the two self-images:

> If I would be with my mother most of the time, you know, would be in the house most of the time doing housework, you know. Not having, you know, not having that much fun as I would, you know, if I would be with them. Riding around, getting high, you know, selling herb (marijuana), all of that . . . I would feel like a little kid, like a little kid washing dishes, cleaning house, stuff like that . . . I'd clean the house if I needed some money she would give it to me.

> I: So, your life inside the house and outside was very different.
> S: Yeah, I feel like, you know, I feel like I ain't having no fun or nothing, you know, all stuck up in the house, I feel different, you know. They (the gang) out there having fun, I'm in there washing dishes . . . I'd tell the time, rush go outside, you know, have some fun. I say, "Damn, I never have fun in the house, but it seems like all the time I go outside I have fun . . . I feel alive when I'm outside . . . in the house I'm all hemmed up."

Much of the draw of the gang was the excitement and the competition among the boys to get attention by showing off.

> You know, you know, I was just thinking 'bout hanging with my friends, you know, getting money, proving to them that I could make more money than them. Prove to them that I got money and stuff like that . . . Getting something better than them. If they get a moped, I get a better moped. They get a bike, I get a better bike. I ain't steal, I only stole one car and I stop. That's too quick, fuck that, I'll get my own car. I said, "No, I can't steal cars."

But on one occasion he did steal a car. Sly felt as though he had to not only equal, but surpass the deviant achievements of the other gang members. The ante for this game of chance continued to get higher and higher. Such coups and feats provided Sly with a sense of being a star and gave him the stature and self-esteem that he so deeply wanted and needed.

Sly loved to be the center of attention. He lapped up the admiring comments made by the witnesses to his exploits topped off when they asked enviously, "How does he steal cars so easily?"

I: You were a bad dude. What do you think you were doing?

S: I don't know. From the first time, man, I started doing what they (street gang members) were doing. I thought I was hot stuff. Really. I look at it now. All the trouble I've been in from the first beginning to this point, like it builds up. Like it builds up if you start stealing from stores like candy and stuff. You say, "Wow, I got over on this," you know, and go higher, steal bikes. Then I got over on this, these mopeds. I got over this, then steal a car . . . That's how it works, man . . . I tried to be Mr. Bigshot, "Look at this moped, $560," you know . . . That's how I probably stealing same. "How does he steal cars so easily?" Then I hot wired and they said "Sly got a car." "Anybody want a ride?"

Here, again, Sly was searching for the affirmation of others to make him feel good, relying on the outside world to mirror back an aggrandized image of himself: "Mr. Bigshot." Something had evidently gone wrong in his early years when he was putting together the foundation of his self-esteem.

The influence that the gang had on Sly's delinquent behavior stemmed largely from his own personal dynamics. Because he did not want these older boys to view him as being a "punk" or as "corny"—threats to his ideal self-image—he tended to go along with the group's antisocial activities, although sometimes quite reluctantly. Actually he realized how much he depended on their acceptance of him. He tried to explain why he allowed himself to be "conned into doing things I ain't suppose to do."

S: I don't know, showing them that I ain't scared to do it, you know, I ain't no punk, you know, stuff like that. Show them that, you know, I ain't no kid, that you know, I could get over just like they can, you know. Show them that, you know, by saying, "I ain't gonna' do it," you know. Show them that I would rather hang with the older ones than the younger ones.

I: So, by what means did you prove to them that you were a man, that you were not a kid?

S: You know, by breaking in, you know, doing B and E's, you know, getting some money, having some money in my pocket, they have some too. Go out partying and all of that. 'Cause, like, they would have mopeds and, you know, and I'd say, "Where you get that moped from?" They say, "I stole it." They say, "You wanna' get one?" I say, "Yeah, man!" You know, hang out with them, you know, rob with them. Then I go steal one, ride around couple hours, then, you know, dump it, you know.

I: So, you would ride around for 2 hours, then just dump it?

S: You know, have it for a while, you know, ride around have some fun (laughs), you know, mess with the girls. Give them rides and stuff, "Sly, give me a ride. If you give me a ride you get this," you know . . . meeting up, meet girls 'cause that's the way you, you know, can check out girls, you know. Having a moped, they all the time want a ride.

Although Sly enjoyed rapping about these thefts, the joy rides, and the girls, he was aware that he had paid dearly for associating with the gang. In his sentence completion responses, this theme was reiterated. To item 3 he said, "A large crowd *is often bad.*" To item 14, he responded, "It is easy to get into trouble when *you're with a lot of people.*" His response to item 66 was, "It hurts when *you get into trouble.*"

Being an active member of the gang was associated with the trouble he found himself involved with day-to-day. It was as if one part of him saw what was happening and the other part of him was seduced by the excitement and attention derived from the deviant escapades he was taught by the older boys. Nor were the relationships with the friends he made in the gang all good. In response to item 13 of the Sentence Completion Test, Sly revealed that he felt betrayed by some of them: "One's closest friends *run over you, mess with you.*" Sly's sense of being with the gang members, yet not entirely of them was reflected in his story to TAT card 9BM:

> Guess all of them, at the beginning, look like all of them got drunk, just laid against each other. And in the middle, I guess he just watching them, you know, just staring at them, looking at them sleeping. At the end, I guess he probably went to sleep, him right there. (Which one?) This one. (The one on the left?) Yeah. (With his back towards you?) Yeah.

In this story Sly separated one figure from the rest of the group. While they slept, he was awake and watching them, staring at them in their drunken (deviant?) slumber. While they were supporting each other, evidently they were not supporting him.

Sly continued in discussing the importance of his friends in his acquisition of a sense of selfhood:

> S: You know, my friends, you know, 'cause I be with them a lot of times and, you know, I hate, you know, being without them, you know. I would feel funny, you know, without being around them.
> I: What would it feel like not being around them?
> S: It would feel funny, you know, I feel I'm lost, I'm in a lost world, you know. Like, every, like behind closed doors or something. That's how I would feel.

This same theme of feeling lost appeared in Sly's story to TAT card 20.

> This one, it looks like he (laughs) is in a lost world. I don't know. He probably just roaming the streets at night thinking about what he gonna' do or think-

ing 'bout his wife or the children, kids are little. Looks like he just strolling around, seeing what he wants to do. At the end, I guess, he probably just left then and went back home or something. Talk to his wife and kids. That's all.

In this story about a person "in a lost world," Sly attributed to the man his own sense of detachment from everything familiar. It was he who was "probably just roaming the streets at night thinking about what he gonna' do." Unlike this man, however, Sly had nobody at home to whom he was truly close. In the lost world inhabited by Sly, he was disconnected not only from bonds of family but also from his own self. Although he often turned to his friends for some relief from these feelings of not belonging anywhere, they could alleviate his sense of emptiness and detachment only temporarily.

Sly's undeveloped sense of personal identity was demonstrated in his Draw-A-Person production. The person he drew was conceived in exceedingly primitive terms, virtually a stick figure except for the facial features and hair. The elements of the human form were those that a young child might create: unidimensional arms and legs, with hands and fingers represented as three prongs and feet drawn as short sticks turned outward at right angles to the legs. The head was attached directly to the body without benefit of a neck, and the figure as a whole was suspended in midair. Although the figure lacked definitive sexual characteristics, Sly said it was a woman and added this comment: "Curly hair, curly head, curly hair, eyes low, hands low. Got on, what's that, farmer's suit. That's it." This was the production of a 17-year-old who had only the barest rudiments of a mature self.

It was as if Sly knew that he had been denied something very crucial at an

FIGURE 4.
Sly's First Drawing for the Draw-A-Person Test.

early age, something he kept searching for and failed to find. In his story in response to TAT card 5, he described the figure as a woman who discovered that something was missing when she looked inside the door:

> Maybe at the beginning, look like she just open the door and look like she got uhm, look like she mad about something. I don't know, the way it looks it look like, I don't know, guess she probably see something that's missing, I don't know. Something probably got stolen or something look strange to her; she trying to figure out what it is. And the end, I guess she found out. (What did she find out?) That something was missing and something was gone or she thought she saw, I don't know. Something that was, I can't put it in the right words. Something that was there, but, oh, I know, it look like in the end, like, probably something that was there got changed around or something. That's how I see that one.

The person in this story may have represented Sly and his sense that something had disappeared or changed in his life or even been stolen from him. There had been an incomprehensible (to him) change at some early point in his life, after which "something that was there" was no longer there. What was it that used to be in Sly's life and then at some point had changed in a way he could not put into words? Although he could not formulate the nature of the loss in specific terms, he could symbolize it in a story like this. Considering his almost insatiable need for the immediate gratification of his desires, which he would not postpone but would satisfy by stealing, it seemed likely that he had failed to move beyond the stage of primary omnipotence (Winnicott, 1971). Rather than learning gradually to restrain his infantile demands he may have experienced an abrupt and harsh disciplining early in life. If there was a sudden cutting off of the gratification of his omnipotent appetite, that experience would have interfered with his ability to make the move to the developmental stage during which the infant learns to tolerate longer and longer delays in getting satisfaction. The symbiotic bond to his mother had been rudely broken, and Sly was left mired in his insatiability, never having shifted to engaging in the instrumental activities to achieve the goals he desired. Everything had been in order and then everything changed. And Sly could not make sense of what had happened. All he knew was that he felt a need which was beyond his control to get what he wanted when he wanted it. Sly was stranded in his early stage of omnipotence, sensing vaguely that something had gone awry and still struggling with the feeling that his mother was withholding something from him.

SLY'S SEARCH FOR A GOOD FATHER

Before being incarcerated Sly used the members of the gang as mirrors that reflected a positive image of himself, but his inclination to look for affirmation did not cease when he was locked up. At the penal facility he found a number of adult males on the staff to whom he responded positively and looked up to for direction. In fact, his willingness to take orders from these men paid off during an incident in which he came very close to forfeiting a long awaited visit home. Under attack by a fellow detainee, Sly was on the brink of retaliating, If it had not been for the presence of a male officer, Mr. Smith, who cooled him down, the weekend pass would have been denied him. Sly described what took place:

> Mr. Smith said, "Sly, just sit down, just ignore it," you know, "ain't no sense in going there and hit him, then you really gonna' lose it." So, I said, "All right," I just sat down.

I: What do you think would have happened if Mr. Smith didn't tell you to sit down?

S: I would have run over and hit him. I wasn't even thinking, I was just thinking, you know, 'bout saying that, you know, "Wow, man, I could, this the opportunity, I really could of went home and now I gotta' wait a week," you know. Then I said, then I thought about it, you know, after he had made me sit down, you know. I thought about it, I said, "I better cool out, you know, for a week," I know a week, I could wait a week. Saturday, yeah, I'm going home.

I: So, you could have blown the whole thing?

S: Yeah, if I would have ran, if Mr. Smith didn't grab me, I probably would have hit him.

Sly shed some light on how differently he conducted himself when under the authority of a man as opposed to a woman. Referring to a male teacher, Mr. Fuma, to whose class in the detention facility he had been transferred from Mrs. Copper's class, Sly said:

> I get along with him all right, but Mrs. Copper, you know, whenever she did something seem like she be doing it on spite and I'd say something about it, you know . . . If he tell me stop talking, I'll stop talking, you know, and don't say nothing.

I: You make it sound as though you give Mr. Fuma more respect than you give Mrs. Copper.

S: I know, you know, Mr. Fuma has respect for me and I know Mrs. Copper probably don't.

However true or false these perceptions of the adults in charge of him happened to be, Sly was unwilling to give the female the benefit of the doubt. The confidence he so readily indicated that he could automatically trust men to treat him fairly enabled Sly to respond less defensively to them than to women. Beyond the matter of trust, Sly's extreme need to identify with men and to feel they respected him was apparent in the warm feelings he expressed about three of the staffers who were males, "The only ones I like is Mr. Brown, Mr. Smith, and Mr. Fuma. They try to help you if you talk to them." With one of them, Mr. Brown, he identified with more closely than any other man he had ever known:

> We cool 'cause, like we talk. He'll ask me, he'll come in like on Saturday and ask me, like, "Sly, how have things been going on?" He is the only one that will ask me . . . he won't ask nobody else. He ask me, "Sly, anything happen in the cottage?" . . . I tell if a fight happened or such and so . . . he nice, thick me and him, he nice to me. That's why I don't like for people try fuck over him when he ain't here, talk 'bout him and all that shit. And when he come they be quiet as a quack, a cat. They'll talk behind his back but don't talk in front of his face 'cause they know what he'll do . . . I get along with him all the time. He bring me stuff from the Campus Shop (canteen) so I help him out . . . sometimes I ask him if he want something from the Campus Shop and I buy him a soda . . . He's all right . . . He tries to help me.

Sly wanted to believe that he and his father would have shared a special relationship similar to the close bond he felt for the officer:

> And my father, like, like, if my father was like Mr. Brown, he'll just go straight out, you know, "Just stay out of trouble, don't be fighting," something like that. If he tell me to stay out of trouble I usually seldom get into trouble. He be mad, too, if I got in trouble he'd say, "Damn, Sly, I just told you," you know, "if she be ready to write you up just cool out and go ahead and do your work." Say, "Sly, the best I can say for you is to switch classes." I got my class switched. And, so he ask me how I'm doing in Mr. Fuma's class. And I said, "All right. I ain't got wrote up yet." And then he said, "I told you, if you get switched you'll be doing all right." And that's what happened.

In Mr. Brown Sly found the strong father figure he had been looking for, a man he thought cared for him in a special way. Sly said that he felt good when Mr. Brown would get angry, further substantiating the existence of his great need to have a man set boundaries for him and thereby indicate to Sly that he was worthwhile. Mr. Brown was the incarnation of the good, attentive father, even on a part-time basis whom Sly had dreamt of having but never had. Once he knew he had the security of this special relationship with Mr. Brown, Sly was able to stay out of trouble during the month that remained of his time to be spent in the penal facility. He now felt more whole than at any other time in his life.

OVERVIEW: SLY'S PSYCHOLOGICAL WORLD

Sly had a driving need for attention and applause. According to his own accounts of the activities of his gang, he was the one who played the lead part in their delinquent escapades. When he stole a moped or a car, the others would say, "Wow, Sly got a car." He was the "Mr. Bigshot" who would go to great lengths to be in the limelight. When he committed crimes, it was not so much for the purpose of acquiring a prized item as it was to show off his daring to the audience in the street and bask in the warmth of their admiration. He fed on their approval. As he put it, "It made me feel good." The girls could even be enticed into taking a ride with him on a stolen moped. After a few hours of joy riding, when the novelty and excitement had worn off, he simply discarded the vehicle. The magic for Sly in putting on a performance was that he could become another person while he acted the part. He could be Superman, the movie star of his own script.

At the same time Sly could not always control the response—the applause cards—to satisfy his hunger for approval: Sometimes he was relegated to being a bit player instead of the lead and he frequently received critical reviews of his act, particularly from adults. Not being the object of special attention was unbearable for him. With his teachers, for example, he had to be the pet. When he failed to gain this special place with them, he made trouble in the classroom and refused to do his work. At the penal institution he badgered his female teacher for not looking at things from his point of view, but as soon as she had him sit next to her, he was all smiles over their special relationship: "I sit by her desk, I be doing my work, she be helping me out. She's all right now." Once he had managed to get her attention focused back on himself and put an end to her critical remarks, he was walking on a cloud. It was always the other person—not he—who had to change their attitude towards him from negative to positive. In his view, a problem in a relationship was never basically his fault.

In this enormous dependence on others to make him feel either very good or very bad about himself, Sly displayed his own emptiness. When the mask of the entertainer was torn away, he was left with very little of his own internalized self-esteem. It required the affirmation of other people flowing directly into the self to make him feel as though he was somebody. It meant that Sly had an insatiable appetite for admiration—a constant need for narcissistic mirroring of the self even though the beautiful reflection was only an illusion. Concerning narcissism and related exhibitionism, Kohut (1971) suggested that they had their source in some early developmental trauma:

> Under favorable circumstances (appropriately selective parental response to the child's demands for an echo to and a participation in the narcissistic-exhibitionistic manifestations of his grandiose fantasies) the child learns to accept his realistic limitations, the grandiose fantasies and the crude exhibitionistic demands are

given up, and are *pari passu* replaced . . . by pleasure in his functions and activities and by realistic self-esteem . . . the outcome of the development of the grandiose self is determined not only by the features of the child's own narcissism but also by certain features of the important personalities who surround the child. (p. 107)

There well may have been a real question in Sly's mind as to whether he was lovable or not. In his narcissism he engaged in a kind of pathological love of himself that he had evidently not been able to gain from the significant others in his early life. The narcissism was compensatory for the feelings that he was nobody, for the suspicions that he was unlovable. Being regarded as a star by his friends gave him a sense of identity, enabling him to feel like a person behind the false front.

But when he was at home there was no one who would do that affirming and mirroring he needed. There he felt unimportant, hemmed in by his mother's rules and her attempts to keep him in the house doing menial household chores. In addition, she denied his requests for things he wanted such as new clothing and money. Quick to anger at being refused the things he knew she was unable to give him, he would go out and steal a purse or get the gang together to break into somebody's house. It appeared that Sly had almost no ability to delay the gratification of his wishes. If he wanted something, it should be there immediately. Although his mother told him repeatedly that he should go out and work if he wanted to have money in his pocket, he was unwilling to take the concrete steps that would bring about the desired goal of paying his own way. It was as though he was an infant who expected instantaneous gratification of his desires and had not yet learned to tolerate longer and longer delays in reaching his goals. He could not cope with the sense of frustration engendered by having to postpone the fulfillment of his smallest wish.

Something had apparently gone wrong in Sly's early emotional development. He had ended up in adolescence still carrying on as though he were in the stage of infantile omnipotence. Concerning the baby's passage from this stage of magical control to "objective perception based on reality testing," Winnicott (1971) wrote:

> *If all goes well* the infant can actually come to gain from the experience of frustration, since incomplete adaptation to need makes objects real, that is to say, hated as well as loved. The consequence of this is that *if all goes well* the infant can be disturbed by a close adaptation to need that is continued too long, not allowed its natural decrease, since exact adaptation resembles magic and the object that behaves *perfectly* becomes no better than an hallucination. Nevertheless, *at the start* adaptation needs to be almost exact, and unless this is so it is not possible for the infant to begin to develop a capacity to experience a relationship to external reality, or even to form a conception of external reality. (p. 11)

In Sly's development, all had not gone well. In fact, he himself sensed that something was amiss, although he could not put it into words. He entertained doubts about whether his mother really loved him. How could she call the cops in to arrest him if she really cared for him? The question seemed to plague him even though he could reason out the answer that she was doing it for his own good. It was possible that the symbiotic bond to his mother was never established or that his infantile omnipotence had been harshly crushed, that he had not been eased gradually enough into the experience that there was a time limit to frustration which was short at first and could be endured for longer and longer periods. Winnicott (1971) stated:

> This problem, which undoubtedly concerns the human infant in an hidden way at the beginning, gradually becomes an obvious problem on account of the fact that the mother's main task (next to providing opportunity for illusion) is disillusionment . . . If things go well, in this gradual disillusionment process, the stage is set for the frustrations that we gather together under the word weaning. (p. 13)

Possibly Sly had been spoiled. Whether he had been overindulged or too strictly disciplined, Sly had not been effectively initiated into the task of reality-acceptance at the early critical phase. An indication of his inability to accept things as they were was reflected in his dream that he could convert his absent and inattentive father into a nurturing parent. This was a part of Sly's larger quest for a responsive and admiring audience to fill up his empty self.

5

Black Delinquent Behavior:
Social and Clinical Issues

Raising black children in the American social context involves many difficulties beyond the usual ones encountered by all parents. But the task is a more arduous one for those parents who are lower class, and even more so in families where the mother is the single parent and breadwinner. During those early weeks of life when infants need continuous care from one mothering person to provide the newborn with stability, they frequently are denied the security of a close mother-infant relationship. Both pregnancy and the care of a demanding baby are too burdensome to an already exhausted woman for her to respond adequately. In addition to shortchanging her new baby in terms of time and attention, the mother may resent his arrival deeply, in part because it can cause a rift between herself and her husband or boyfriend. Typically, it has been the father who leaves when there is marital or relationship discord, and the mother is therefore compelled to take care of the baby and his siblings alone. If problems between the parents are not solved, the child may have little or no contact with the father after his departure.

MOTHER AS SOCIAL AGENT

People are quick to place the blame for children getting into trouble on the shoulders of mothers who are raising their children alone—and these women know how the society regards them. What is frequently overlooked is that most of these women are attempting to be effective parents but their efforts are undermined by social conditions beyond their control. Their lives are based on a quicksand of insecurities, both financial and emotional. All too frequently their own children fail to comprehend the emotional and physical struggles they are engaged in—and their sons often add even more grief to their mothers' lives by getting into trouble. Feeling they have failed as parents and even harboring deep emotions of shame, such mothers begin to define themselves as powerless to bring about change in the lives of their errant sons. As a last resort—and knowing full well the injustices that have been perpetrated against black folk by white institutions, they sometimes give in to the truly desperate act of calling the police to put their sons in jail. Unfortunately, the fantasy that the penal system will in some way magically change their man-child and eliminate his deviant behavior never becomes a reality.

At times these women entertain thoughts of escaping—of just running away from their heavy burdens of being cast in the role of both parents to their sons. With such incredible demands on the mother to respond to the emotional and material needs of her children, she herself has no one to lean on. Having almost none of her own needs met, she is in a poor position to meet the needs of those in her family who are depending on her emotionally and also expecting her to fulfill their desires to own the material goods that are dangled in front of them by an affluent, white society.

The black inner city communities across the country are teeming with women who are working diligently to better their personal and family circumstances. Attempting to raise families on their meager earnings or welfare payments, they are judicious in the use of their monies. Although they are watching every penny, their children want money to buy the attractive consumer goods advertised on television—all those expensive things that are supposed to make people beautiful and happy. Poor black folks want to be pretty and joyful, too, and youngsters are easy prey to the blandishments of the media without having the means to acquire what they are being taught they should possess in order to feel good about themselves.

The mother in this social context is forced into the role of being the agent of material and psychological deprivation to her children. Because of her lack of success the boy begins to have real questions about her real worth as a person. Parents are supposed to be the providers of the Good Life. Because of his growing lack of respect for her he cannot follow what she says. He starts to see his mother's "solution"—hard work and being law abiding—as a pipe dream at best. Because he is not caught up in his mother's almost compulsive attempt to "make it" in this way, he is more able to be objective and recognize the losing battle in which she is engaged. With his own limited access to economic resources and her inability to supply them, he finds other means to taste the sweeter life. The fun and excitement of shoplifting a candy bar can lead to the greater joy of stealing a moped. Having the support of friends in a gang to steal what they are unable to buy for themselves both reinforces the deviant behavior pattern and provides a real sense of group solidarity, a feeling that is absent in his response to his family relationships.

The social context of the black ghetto involves pressures on families, which often lead to disruptions in the relations between parents and children. Frequently a boy's personal struggle to become a man takes place under socioeconomic conditions that encourage husbands and fathers to leave home. Under ideal conditions a son's relationship and identification with his father assist him in differentiating himself from the primary symbiosis with the mother. A home without a father deprives the son of this much needed assistance and may force him to rely on other methods of asserting his separateness, e.g., rebellious delinquent acts. Another factor often interferes with the move to individuate. With the fathers gone, the mothers find themselves having to play the roles of both parents, including the disciplining of their sons. Their assertive methods of discipline seem to drive their sons away from them and toward macho images of men along with the aggressive, socially deviant behavior of such men whose antisocial patterns of life are also adopted by street gangs.

DELINQUENT BEHAVIOR AND PSYCHOLOGICAL DEVELOPMENT

In our explorations of the psychological worlds of Jerome, Pete, and Sly, a good deal of the evidence was found that a disturbance in the mother–son relationship had played some considerable part in their motivation for delinquent behavior. In addition, the absence of the father was in all three cases significantly related to the appearance of delinquency. Each boy had been raised by his mother after there had been domestic difficulties between his parents that had led to the father leaving the family unit. In a general sense, the boys' antisocial acts could be interpreted as troubled expressions of their attempts to dis-identify with their mothers and identify with men. Unlike a girl whose gender identity is virtually assured when reared by a woman, a boy must dis-identify with his mother *and* then identify with a male figure (counteridentification with women). According to Greenson (1968), a boy must:

> Renounce the pleasure and security-giving closeness that identification with the mothering person affords, and he must form an identification with the less accessible father. The outcome will be determined by several elements. The mother must be willing to allow the boy to identify with the father figure. She can facilitate this by genuinely enjoying and admiring the boy's boyish features and skills and must look forward to his further development along this line. (p. 373)

But when the father is absent and the mother is beset with the pressures of rearing children in circumstances where she herself may be desperately short of emotional support, the problems encountered by a boy are compounded. The sons may make attempts to identify with male models outside the home who symbolize the most raw, naked, and extreme forms of masculine behavior— fighting, sexual conquest of women, defiance and disrespect for law and order, destructiveness, and living without encumbrances. Adopting such supermasculine behavior is a manifestation of the striving toward separation-individuation from the mothers who represent the status quo. In many instances, however, the boys also cling to the old mother–son symbiotic tie, feeling ambivalent about shifting their identification from their mothers to men.

The mother may well not understand her son's need to escape from her. The boy, in turn, may not really know how to explain to his mother the attraction he has to the world of tough men, but he instinctively knows that there is something there for him to secure (which he cannot get at home from his mother) if he is to become a man. Jerome, Pete, and Sly, each in his distinctive way, became involved in delinquent behavior in the course of attempting to separate from their mothers.

Jerome: An Ambivalent Bond to the Mother

Jerome's delinquent behavior was deeply embedded in disturbances in his psychological development. In late adolescence he was still struggling with ambivalent feelings toward his mother. On the one hand, he was unable to give up his infantile craving to be physically and emotionally attached to her although on the other hand he wanted desperately to free himself from his dependence on her. One part of him was preoccupied with the idea of securing a close and exclusive place in his mother's affections; the other part of him hated her for never providing the maternal care he had gone without as an infant and young child.

Jerome's developmental difficulties had their origin in the enormous inadequacies of the care given him during the early phases of his life. There was little doubt that he had not received even a minimum level of "good-enough mothering." The situation was that he was never central to the lives of either his natural mother nor the mother surrogate. Neither of these women had responded to his early needs with the willing preoccupation and devotion required for a baby to get a healthy emotional start in life. In fact, they resented having to put up with the trouble he caused them and beat him frequently.

It was not surprising that Jerome had made such poor progress in detaching himself from his mother. Remaining fixated on securing the maternal love he had never known, he wanted to have his mother under his magical control in a position where she catered to his every whine and whimper. As a young adult, he still harbored fantasies of sharing her bed, not with the intention of achieving sexual union with her, but with the far more primitive hope of satisfying his wish for mother–infant symbiosis.

Much of Jerome's delinquent behavior reflected an arrest in the development of the structure of his psychological world. Because he conceived of himself as a "part" of his mother—in the sense of a symbiotic intertwining of an infant with its mother—he regarded her possessions as his and took them from her quite freely. From his infantile perspective, the money in her purse represented symbolically the love and undivided devotion he thought were his rightful due.

When his mother put him out of the house at age 16, Jerome continued to search for a good mother—what he referred to as a "real mother"—who would make him the central focus of her life. When other women—particularly mature women in the helping professions—tried to fill this role, he always resorted to stealing from them when they turned down some minor request. Such incidents of failure to respond to his unbridled demands for nurturing seemed to reawaken the shattering trauma of the denials inflicted on him during his development. Treating these mother substitutes like his mother, he struck back by stealing from them. Even though these women had gone out of their way to be benefactors, Jerome seemed unable to affiliate himself with them for long. His impulsive drive system—like a young child's—tended to govern his behavior to such a degree that he did not foresee the possible consequences of his actions. Any woman who attempted to help him was slated to be a victim of his petty thievery because no one could live up to his high standards of performance for a "real mother."

Although a large part of Jerome's psychic energy was devoted to his ambivalent bond with his mother, a portion of his psychological world involved men. His father had abandoned him. Jerome did not even remember his father and could not admire this man who had allowed his girlfriend to beat him when he was a baby. His mother's boyfriends were seen as rivals for his mother's love, putting him in competition with them in a battle he could not win because his mother did not give him equal access to her. Instead of identifying with men, he regarded them as authority figures to fear and disobey. In the absence of male models with whom to identify, Jerome's task of disidentifying with his mother was made all the more difficult. He ended up feeling deeply distrustful of both men and women—a loner who had never completed the task of developing a sense of his own separateness and individuality.

The delinquent boys who are loners tend to have more troubled developmental histories. When they have been victims of parental neglect, rejection, and/or child abuse, the separation-individuation process is made much more complicated. Although trying to leave behind the "bad mother" who has failed to nurture them, at the same time they cannot actually part from her because they are so desirous of having an idealized one-to-one relationship with her. This ambivalence makes the separation harder to carry out because the boys' hopes are predicated on the unrealizable fantasy that their mothers will be different (accepting and loving) the next time they return home. Consequently the boys find themselves being in constant limbo vis-a-vis her. In their aggressive acts can be seen their feeble and self-destructive attempts to wrest from the world what their mothers never gave them—a true sense of omnipotence (Winnicott, 1965) and a feeling of being loved and cared for. These boys may also see their absent fathers as having a hand in their tragic life circumstances by not being there to protect them.

Pete: A Masculinity–Feminity Conflict

The turning point in Pete's young life, as it was reconstructed in Chapter 3, was the sudden and unexplained departure of his father from what was remembered as a blissfully happy family circle. Until the breakup of his parents' marriage, Pete had thought of himself as his father's favorite child. When the person who had understood him best and loved him most was gone, it was as if Pete was without the psychological mooring he needed to make the next moves in the process of disidentifying with his mother and completing and consolidating his own masculine identity.

Increasingly, Pete idealized the memory of his father as he faced the difficult changes that occurred following the traumatic rupture. Creating an image of the perfect father helped him justify his anger and hostility towards his "stepfather" whom he never accepted as a member of the family. Now, instead of being the favored child, as he thought he was when his father was present, he was assigned the role of a male Cinderella. By the time he was 12, his mother had put him in charge of his younger siblings and eventually gave him full responsibility for performing all the household maintenance tasks and meal preparations. Although he complained bitterly about being treated like a maid and a child, actually he was quite ambivalent about the situation. Part of him wanted desperately to please his mother whereas another part, his emerging masculine self, was struggling against what he felt were her attempts to feminize and infantilize him.

This ambivalence of Pete's may explain why he had to assert his independence from his mother so dramatically in wild and destructive ways. In addition to his difficulties in shedding the image of maid and kid, he had to deal with his concerns about being so short in stature. His acts of violence—assaults on women, breaking and entering, and gang fighting—could be considered his ways of compensating for the weak and passive self contained in the roles of the maid and the little boy.

The street gang Pete belonged to was the social vehicle he used to establish what was not validated about him at home—that he was a real man. The gang members actively promoted his challenges to his mother's restrictions, thereby supporting his efforts to differentiate from her feminine definitions of him. When he joined the other boys in vandalizing someone else's home, he could express his own potency with few inhibitions on his masculine destructive self. He felt exhilarated by his raw power to create disorder and disarray—emotions he hardly dared to contemplate when he was cleaning and polishing the family's apartment. It was in the gang members and their super-masculine style that Pete found his models of masculinity.

Pete had joined a street gang whose members seemed to have done a better job of satisfying each other's needs than their mothers did. In many cases, the street gang became a boy's "new family," because it provided certain forms of nurturing which he craved. However, to be part of a street gang meant a boy had to endorse and carry out various acts of fighting, stealing, and vandalism. Because a ghetto mother feared her son's involvement with these "bad boys" and their violent activities, she tried to keep him at home, thereby impeding his attempts at emancipation. Feeling shackled and emasculated, the boy in turn displaced his intense feelings of anger towards his mother onto other persons and their property.

Although uncertain about his masculinity, Pete was developmentally further along than either Jerome or Sly. One critical reason for his relatively more mature emotional state was seemingly the result of his having had both parents available and at least somewhat nurturant to him until he was 8 years old—the time that his father mysteriously disappeared. Pete's psychological development, as it was reconstructed in the case analysis, became arrested at the point where he was making serious attempts to identify with his father and consolidate a sense of male identity. Nevertheless, unlike Jerome and Sly, he had become able to express his love for another person (as reflected in his relationship with his girl friend, Gloria), indicating some movement towards adulthood.

Sly: A Search for Self-Esteem

As a means of satisfying his hunger for approval, Sly came to practice a kind of crude exhibitionism. In return for the admiring acceptance of his friends, he escalated the seriousness of his delinquent escapades so that he would be seen as the best thief—"baddest dude." When he committed crimes like stealing a moped or a car, it was not in order to own the vehicle or strip it down for cash, but rather to put on a show for the gang members and the girls. He needed to be the star who inspired awe and amazement. Being "Mr. Bigshot" in their eyes afforded him a temporary respite from the otherwise constant void he experienced of feeling like a nobody.

This same enormous need for narcissistic mirroring was present in Sly's other relationships. In his elementary and junior high school classes he recalled that some of the female teachers made him feel inferior and stupid. He reacted by playing hooky—the beginning of his subsequent history of truancy. With a teacher at the reformatory he was angry when he failed to get the preferential treatment he craved from her. When she gave anything less than special attention to his problems, he acted up to draw attention to himself. Once he succeeded in establishing a privileged relationship with her, he settled down and did his work. He demanded—and received for a short period—the narcissistic nurturance that enabled him to feel he had a positive self. Once she slipped back into treating him like the rest of the students, however, he reverted to his well-established pattern of making trouble when he felt slighted.

With his girl friends, Sly seemed to be afraid of the possibility that they might respond to him negatively. He was always on guard not to hurt their feelings. In fact, he had so little self-confidence in these relationships that he could not even bring himself to refuse a request for money he did not have (and therefore was forced to steal). It was evident that he was looking to these young women rather than within himself to validate his sense of self-worth—so much so that he pretended they remained faithful to him during his prison term even though he had quite definitive evidence to the contrary.

Something had happened early in Sly's development to leave him in this state of constant need for narcissistic mirroring. In his narcissism he seemed to be engaged in a kind of infantile love of himself that he had failed to gain from his caretakers as an infant. He kept on trying to compensate for his feelings that he might not be lovable by proving his worth over and over again. Indeed, there was suspicion in Sly's mind that his mother might not really love him. Around her he also demonstrated quite openly his inability to tolerate any delay in the fulfillment of his wishes. Like an infant before weaning, he had not yet learned to wait for what he wanted, but insisted on the instant gratification of his desires. When he asked his mother for something, he expected her to supply it immediately. Furious at being refused, his pattern was to rush out and break into someone's house.

Sly was troubled by the course his life had taken, not knowing where to turn for the love and respect he so deeply craved. The hopes he had placed in renewing his relationship with his father were dashed by his father's unwillingness to keep in touch with him even minimally. Judging from the emotional distance he had felt from his mother, from the time of his earliest memories, it seems likely that the "selfobject bond" (Kohut, 1977) between them had been prematurely ruptured. Sly had reached adolescence burdened with an inability to maintain a feeling of his own self-worth, which he had tried to compensate for in behavior that got him into trouble.

The delinquent behavior of Jerome, Pete, and Sly took place in the context of disarray and instability of their family situations. They lacked the safety of an intact family structure in which they would have had a better chance of establishing a sense of security while dealing with and organizing their destructive inclinations. In a healthy family a mother and father complement each other in such a way that the child is able to integrate his destructive impulses with his loving impulses. This enables him to recognize that destructive ideas are a real part of living and not necessarily dangerous. Winnicott (1973) points out that a "child absolutely requires an environment that is indestructible in essential aspects; certainly carpets get dirtied . . . and an occasional window gets broken but somehow the home sticks together, and behind all this is the confidence that . . . in the relationship between the parents; the family is a going concern" (p. 367).

The broken family structure of our three subjects prohibited the development of any complementary functions between parents. In large measure, their fathers were not only absent, they were completely unavailable. This unavailability made it difficult for their sons to test their aggressive impulses and feel safe in doing so within the home. In fact, the boys often said that their mothers refused to permit any fighting or displays of anger at home. Each one of them lacked a secure home environment in which limits could be tested without risk of the disintegration of the family structure.

In a general way Jerome, Pete, and Sly all shared similar chaotic family circumstances and their antisocial impulses certainly spilled out into the streets. Yet each family was unique and, as a consequence, each of our subjects had unique experiences that are critical to our understanding of the psychological meaning of their acts of delinquency.

PSYCHOTHERAPY FOR BLACK DELINQUENTS

In the summaries of the psychological worlds of three black delinquents, some general commonalities in their life experiences were highlighted. First, their delinquent acts reflected the presence of some developmental problems. In each case, there was evidence that the boy had become fixated at one or another stage of development. The consequences for each one of them was that he was hampered by the inflexibility of his personality structure. Instead of proceeding with the growth toward adulthood, they were caught in the process of repeating immature, self-defeating patterns of behavior. Second, the boys did not understand the source of their antisocial tendencies and aggressive inclinations, although they could describe the specific details of incidents, which had triggered any specific violent acting-out episode. They certainly remembered how they felt while committing such an act. It "made me feel better" was the usual expression. The three boys felt isolated and helpless in dealing with the confused and troubled existence that had been their lot since early childhood. When their antisocial behavior had, in Winnicott's (1973) words, "became a clinical feature and the child became difficult," (p. 366) no one had recognized it as a sign of hope. If the first signals of difficulty had been recognized and treated closer to the time of the early experience, the youngster might have begun to make sense of the undesirable behavior and its origin.

Black youngsters like Jerome, Pete, and Sly have received almost none of this kind of therapeutic treatment at the early stages of their delinquent behavior. In fact, questions have been raised about the ability of lower class blacks (whether adults or youth, nondelinquent or delinquent) to make effective use of psychotherapy even if it were offered to them. Historically, the distribution of mental health services has been class related, with the long-term talking therapies going to the middle and upper classes and the shorter therapies and diagnoses of untreatable psychoses going to poor people (Hollingshead & Redlich, 1958). Inasmuch as blacks fall proportionately in higher numbers among the poor—and not coincidently among the juvenile and adult criminal population—they have neither been given nor taken advantage of extensive treatment for emotional disturbances. Often the situation faced by blacks with psychological difficulties as stated by Jenkins (1982) is that:

> Youngsters and adults alike, are caught as it were between the Scylla of being seen as too disturbed for more prestigious interpersonally oriented therapies and the Charybdis of being seen as not really meriting psychological treatment—as simply manifesting "culturally appropriate" behavior or meriting incarceration. (p. 154)

Jerome, Pete, and Sly and their fellow adolescent inmates have fallen into the rubric of "not really meriting psychological treatment." The psychological services they have received have been confined mainly to classification at in-take and routine group sessions. Would some or all of them benefit from more intensive therapy? In a sense the research interviews resemble the form and substance of clinical interviews enough to permit an assessment of this question. Would they be good candidates or not? The responses of the boys to long-term interviewing could serve as case studies for analyzing how they would perform in therapy.

It is said about lower class clients that they are not verbal and self-observing enough to engage in a therapeutic mode of communication. However, the responses of Jerome, Pete, and Sly to the opportunity to communicate with the interviewer served to belie this argument. When the boys began to feel comfortable and understood, they were quite articulate about their psychological experiences. Indeed, in the course of the interviews for the research, it became clear that they wanted to be heard and assisted in understanding themselves. Not only were they fluent in giving detailed descriptions of their experiences, but their use of metaphors—an indicator of an advanced level of symbolizing—was striking. For example, in describing his fear of his mother, Pete said she could "smack the taste out of my mouth." There was no evidence here of supposed deficiencies in the capacity to communicate adequately in a therapeutic relationship.

Another characteristic of lower class and minority clients, which is said to make them unsuitable for psychological treatment, is their supposed reluctance to disclose painful problems and examine their origins. Although Jerome, Pete, and Sly were somewhat guarded about opening up during their initial interviews, subsequently they were less inclined to hide their inner selves from the interviewer. They talked about issues they had never before shared with anyone. For example,

Jerome confessed that he wanted to sleep beside his mother like a baby. This came out of the mouth of an 18-year-old who presented himself to the world as a lady's man. These teenagers, who typically presented themselves as strong and daring in their delinquent acts, displayed the weaker sides of themselves during the interviews. In this setting they let down their defenses and experienced feelings of doubt, fear, depression, loneliness, and despair—and childish pleasure in their personal triumphs over others.

It is reported that blacks drop out of therapy in the early stages of treatment at a high rate (Sue, McKinney, Allen, & Hall, 1974; Sue, 1977) due to the lack of rapport between the therapist and client. One of the ingredients of this misalliance is the failure of the therapist to express his empathy with the client openly. When dealing with black delinquents, the stance of the therapist must be one of active involvement, making known his concern and caring for the youngster as though he was taking the role of a good parent. Because the young delinquent's attitude towards adults is colored by his negative experiences with his parents and other representatives of authority, a tie with the therapist cannot be established until his mistrust of the therapist is dispelled. The therapist can only win the boy's trust by forging a therapeutic alliance with him that is directed towards actively aiding the youngster in addressing his current difficulties. The adolescent must early on come to feel that he is deriving some concrete benefit from the treatment. The therapist for this type of population must be one who understands that the delinquent's antisocial behavior reflects his unsuccessful attempts to solve deep inner struggles. The goal of the treatment is to help the client become aware of his unconscious impulses and aid him in taking responsibility for his deviant behavior.

Let us turn now to consider how the kind of understanding elaborated in our three case studies may be applied to the problem of devising effective strategies of psychotherapy. In Jerome we see a young man whose subjective world resembles that of an infant with a tremendous need to feel a sense of primary attachment. Therapy in a case such as this one requires a therapist who has enormous tolerance for childish acting out and who is capable of withstanding constant testing. The therapist must also remain fully aware that Jerome, although appearing to be a virile model of masculinity, is emotionally governed by the most primitive of needs. In fact, his delinquent behavior—particularly his stealing—can be understood as an effort to attain the union with a maternal figure that he never adequately experienced in his actual life. The therapist in this situation is in many respects in the role of a surrogate mother and must use the therapeutic bond as a medium for providing forms of care and understanding to Jerome, which his real parents were either unable or unwilling to give. One might anticipate that the therapist's work with him would consist primarily in the task of establishing a relationship in which on the one hand he could begin to experience trust and on the other hand he would gradually learn to accept the limits that are inevitable parts of mature relationships.

In contrast to Jerome's need for attachment, Pete's dominant needs are concerned with the issues of establishing and reinforcing a sense of masculine identity. The therapist working with him should ideally be a male who is secure in his own identity, able to mirror and affirm Pete's healthy strivings for masculine autonomy, and willing ultimately to serve him as a major identification figure. The therapist thus is in the role of a surrogate father, replacing the real father who disappeared during Pete's middle childhood. A critical feature of the therapeutic work would be to assist him in becoming able to let down his super-masculine defense and learn to express his doubts and vulnerabilities without feeling that such expressions are signs of unmanliness and weakness.

The most prominent motivation underlying Sly's delinquent behavior, in contrast to both Jerome and Pete, appears in his indiscriminate all-driving narcissistic need for attention and recognition. One would expect that Sly would attach himself to a therapist quite readily because of the undivided attention such a relationship entails. The therapist, be it a man or a woman, must serve as an admiring object prepared to reflect back Sly's nondelinquent accomplishments and potentialities in a way that makes him feel appreciated and recognized. At the same time, it would be necessary to gently challenge his need to perform heroic feats and help him establish a more genuine, complete, and full sense of self.

Under the best of circumstances this type of intervention is arduous and difficult. If the youngster is black and poor and the therapist is white and middle class, the relationship is loaded with potential for countertransference on the part of the therapist and resistance on the part of the client. A black therapist would not have to deal with the issue of race difference, but the social class disparity would be an obstacle to overcome in establishing a therapeutic relationship. Although Jerome, Pete, and Sly would surely benefit from appropriately structured psychotherapy, there are problems in recruiting therapists who are fully committed to the task of giving adequate forms of treatment to youngsters who, like them, are poor, black, and delinquent.

Appendix A:
Preliminary Questionnaire

1. How long have you been incarcerated?
2. What offense led to you being placed here (at the juvenile penal facility)?
3. When and what was your first offense?
4. How well do you get along with your father?
5. When did you last see your father?
6. How well do you get along with your mother?
7. How would you describe your relationship with your mother?
8. Do you feel that your mother understands you and what life is like for you?
9. Do you think your mother was too strict with you?
10. Did you ever dream of being away from your mother and her influence over you?
11. Was your mother always afraid that you would get into trouble?
12. How do you feel while committing an offense?
13. What is your mother's reaction to your offenses?
14. How do you feel when you are physically close to your mother?
15. Was it okay to openly get angry with your mother for something she did to you?
16. If not, how would you express your anger so that she did not know about it?
17. Is there something you would like from your mother that she has never given you?
18. If you could be anything in the world what would that be?

Appendix B:
Description of Thematic
Apperception Test Cards

1: A young boy is looking at a violin that is on a table before him.

3BM: Located on the floor adjacent to a couch is a boy with his head resting on his right arm. On the floor beside him is a handgun.

4: A middle-aged woman is grabbing the shoulder of a middle-aged man whose face is positioned as though he is pulling away from her.

5: A middle-aged woman is peering into a room from the threshold of a half-opened door.

6BM: A small elderly woman stands with her back to a tall young man. The young man has a puzzled look on his face, which is cast downward.

7BM: A man with gray hair is looking toward a younger man who is staring into the distance.

8BM: An adolescent boy looks from the picture. On one side the barrel of a rifle is seen; the scene of a surgical operation is located in the background.

9BM: Four men dressed in overalls are lying down in a grassy area.

12M: A young man with closed eyes is reclined on a couch. A thin elderly man is leaning over the former figure with his hand stretched above the other's face.

13MF: Standing in the foreground is a young man with a downcast head lodged in his arm. Behind him is a woman who is lying on a bed.

14: The silhouette of a figure against a window. The remaining part of the picture is completely black.

15: An emaciated man with closed hands is standing among tombstones.

16: A blank white card.

17BM: A nude man is holding onto a rope. He is either climbing down or up the rope.

18BM: A man is grabbed from behind by three hands. Those grabbing him are not visible.

129

18GF: A woman with her hands around the neck of another woman whom she seems to be pushing backward over a stairway bannister.

20:   A dimly lighted figure leaning against a lamppost during the dark of night.

References

Ackerly, S. Rebellion and its relation to delinquency and neurosis in sixty adolescents. *American Journal of Orthopsychiatry,* 1933, *3,* 147-160.

Aichhorn, A. *Wayward youth.* New York: Viking Press, 1935.

Allport, G. W. *Pattern and growth in personality.* New York: Holt, Rinehart, & Winston, 1961.

Ausubel, D. P. Problems of adolescent adjustment. *Bulletin of the National Association of Secondary School Principals,* 1950, *34,* 1-84.

Bandura, A., & Walters, R. H. *Adolescent aggression.* New York: Ronald Press, 1959.

Bellak, L. *The Thematic Apperception Test, the Children's Apperception Test and the Senior Apperception Technique in Clinical Use* (3rd Ed.). New York: Grune & Stratton, 1975.

Bernstein, B. Social class, speech systems, and psychotherapy. *British Journal of Sociology,* 1964, *15,* 54-64.

Blos, P. *The young adolescent: Clinical studies.* New York: The Free Press, 1970.

Blos, P. *The adolescent passage: Developmental issues.* New York: International Universities Press, 1979.

Bredemeier, H. C. The socially handicapped and the agencies: A social market analysis. In F. Riessman, J. Cohen, & A. Pearl (Eds.), *Mental health of the poor.* New York: The Free Press, 1964.

Cloward, R. A. Illegitimate means, anomie and deviant behavior. *American Sociological Review,* 1959, *24,* 164-176.

Cloward, R. A., & Ohlin, L. E. *Delinquency and opportunity: A theory of delinquent gangs.* New York: The Free Press, 1960.

Cohen, A. K. *Delinquent boys: The culture of the gang.* New York: The Free Press, 1955.

Criminal Victimization in the United States, 1981. National Crime Survey Report, NCJ-90208, November 1983. United States Department of Justice, Bureau of Justice Statistics, Washington, D.C.

Diller, V. *The Ballet Dancer: In-depth psychobiographical case studies.* (Doctoral Dissertation, Yeshiva University, 1979).

131

Gans, H. J. Social and physical planning for the elimination of urban poverty. *Washington University Law Quarterly*, 1963, 2–18.

Gordon, J. E. Project CAUSE, the federal anti-poverty program, and some implications of subprofessional training. *American Psychologist*, 1965, *20*, 334–343.

Gough, H. G., & Peterson, D. The identification and measurement of predispositional factors in crime and delinquency. *Journal of Consulting Psychology*, 1952, *16*, 207–212.

Greenson, R. R. Dis-identifying from mother: Its special importance for the boy. *International Journal of Psycho-Analysis*, 1968, *49*, 370–373.

Grossbard, H. Ego deficiency in delinquents. *Social Casework*, 1962, *43*, 171–178.

Healy, W., & Bronner, A. F. *Delinquents and criminals, their making and unmaking: Studies in two american cities.* New York: MacMillan, 1926.

Healy, W., & Bronner, A. F. *New light on delinquency and its treatment.* New Haven, CT: Yale University Press, 1936.

Hearings, Criminal Justice Subcommittee, House Judiciary Committee, 1984. Conducted by the Subcommittee on Criminal Justice of the Committee on the Judiciary, United States House of Representatives, Ninety-eighth Congress, Second Session, October 1984. Representative John Conyers, Jr., Michigan, Chairman. U. S. House of Representatives Hearing H-522-16.

Hewitt, L. E., & Jenkins, R. L. *Fundamental patterns of adjustment: The dynamics of their origin.* Springfield, IL: State of Illinois, 1947.

Hollingshead, A. B., & Redlich, F. C. *Social class and mental illness.* New York: Wiley, 1958.

Holsapple, J. Q., & Miale, F. R. *Sentence completion—A projective method for the study of personality.* Springfield, IL: Thomas, 1954.

Hunter, D. R. Slums and social work or wishes and the double negative. In B. Rosenberg, I. Gerver, & F. W. Howton (Eds.), *Mass society in crisis: Social problems and social pathology.* New York: MacMillan, 1964.

Jenkins, A. H. *The psychology of the Afro-American: A humanistic approach.* New York: Pergamon Press, 1982.

Jenkins, R. L., & Glickman, S. Patterns of personality organization among delinquents. *The Nervous Child*, 1947, *6*, 329–339.

Johnson, A. M. Sanctions for superego lacunae of adolescents. In K. R. Eissler (Ed.), *Searchlights on delinquency.* New York: International Universities Press, 1949.

Johnson, A. M., & Szurek, S. A. The genesis of antisocial acting out in children and adults. *Psychoanalysis Quarterly*, 1952, *21*, 323–343.

Kohut, H. *The analysis of the self—A systematic approach to the psychoanalytic treatment of narcissistic personality disorders.* New York: International Universities Press, 1971.

Kohut, H. *The restoration of the self.* New York: International Universities Press, 1977.

Mahler, M. S., Pine, F., & Bergman, A. *The psychological birth of the human infant: Symbiosis and individuation.* New York: Basic Books, 1975.

McMahon, J. T. The working class psychiatric patient: A clinical view. In F. Riessman, J. Cohen, & A. Pearl (Eds.), *Mental health of the poor.* New York: The Free Press, 1964.

McWilliams, N. Helpers: A study in normal personality. Doctoral Dissertation, Rutgers University, 1976. *Dissertation Abstract International,* 1976, *37*(6), 31556-B. (University Microfilms No. 76-27, 025).

Merton, R. K. Social structure and anomie. *American Sociological Review,* 1938, *3,* 672-682.

Merton, R. K. *Social theory and social structure.* Glencoe, IL: The Free Press, 1957.

Miller, W. B. Lower class culture as a generating milieu of gang delinquency. *Journal of Social Issues,* 1958, *15,* 5-19.

Minuchin, S. & Fishman, H. C. *Family therapy techniques.* Cambridge, MA: Harvard University Press, 1981.

Minuchin, S., Montalvo, B., Guerney, B. G., Jr., Rosman, B. L., and Schumer, F. *Families of the slums: An exploration of their structure and treatment.* New York: Basic Books, 1967.

Murray, H. A. *Explorations in personality.* New York: Oxford University Press, 1938.

Muus, R. E. Peter Blos' modern psychoanalytic interpretation of adolescence. *Journal of Adolescence,* 1980, *3,* 229-252.

Offer, D., Marohn, R. C., & Ostrov, E. *The psychological world of the juvenile delinquent.* New York: Basic Books, 1979.

Peterson, D. R., Quay, H. C., & Cameron, G. R. Personality and background factors in juvenile delinquency as inferred from questionnaire responses. *Journal of Consulting Psychology,* 1959, *23,* 395-399.

Peterson, D. R., Quay, H. C., & Tiffany, T. L. Personality factors related to juvenile delinquency. *Child Development,* 1961, *32,* 355-372.

Quay, H. C. & Peterson, D. R. A brief scale for juvenile delinquency. *Journal of Clinical Psychology,* 1958, *14,* 139-142.

Reckless, W. C., & Dinitz, S. Self-concept and delinquency. *Journal of Criminal Law, Criminology and Police Science,* 1967, *58,* 515-523.

Redl, F., & Wineman, D. *Children Who hate: The disorganization and breakdown of behavior controls.* Glencoe, IL: The Free Press, 1951.

Stolorow, R., & Atwood, G. *Faces in the cloud: Subjectivity in personality theory.* New York: Jason Aronson, 1979.

Stolorow, R., & Lachman, F. M. *Psychoanalysis of developmental arrests: Theory and treatment.* New York: International Universities Press, 1980.

Sue, S. Community mental health services to minority groups: Some optimism, some pessimism. *American Psychologist,* 1977, *32,* 616-624.

Sue, S., McKinney, H., Allen, D., & Hall, J. Delivery of community mental health services to black and white clients. *Journal of Consulting and Clinical Psychology,* 1974, *42,* 794-801.

Tiffany, T. L., Peterson, D. R., & Quay, H. C. Types and traits in the study of juvenile delinquency. *Journal of Clinical Psychology,* 1961, *17,* 19-24.

Uniform Crime Reports for the United States, 1984, Table 36. Federal Bureau of Investigation, United States Department of Justice. Washington, DC, 1985, 175.

Visotsky, H. M. Approaches to the treatment of the socially deprived and culturally different. In *Social Work Practice, 1963: Selected Papers, 90th Annual Forum, National Conference on Social Welfare.* New York: Columbia University Press, 1963.

White, R. W. *Lives in progress: A study of the natural growth of personality.* New York: Holt, Rinehart, & Winston, 1952.

White, R. W. *The study of lives: Essays in personality in honor of Henry A. Murray.* New York: Holt, Rinehart, & Winston, 1953.

Winnicott, D. W. *The maturational processes and the facilitating environment.* New York: International Universities Press, 1965.

Winnicott, D. W. *Playing and reality.* New York: Basic Books, 1971.

Winnicott, D. W. Delinquency as a sign of hope. In S. Feinstein & P. Giovachinni (Eds.), *Adolescent psychiatry.* New York: Basic Books, 1973.

Author Index

Subject Index

Abuse, child, 18, 30, 38, 39, 51-52, 54, 66, 71, 94, 118
Adolescence, 69, 71-72, 80, 87-89, 112, 124, 125
Aggression, 27, 42, 54, 59-60, 68, 74-78, 89, 92, 117, 120, 122, 123
Alcohol abuse, 6, 12, 46
Anger, 24-25, 27, 28, 38, 40, 54, 66, 71, 74-77, 94-95, 98, 103, 112, 121
Anxiety, 76
Arrested psychological development, 30, 50-51, 118
Aspirations, 44-45, 82
Autonomy, *see* Separation

Betrayal, 43, 54, 85
Blaming the victim, 4
Breaking and entering, 50, 59, 75-76, 89, 92, 94, 105
Breast, 51
Breuer, 14
Brutality, police, *see* Police, brutality

Case study method, 10, 13, 14, 16
Children Who Hate, 11
Correctional programs, 19-22
Counselors, 21, 29
    male, 40-41
    as mother-substitutes, 30-31, 119
    sexual feelings toward, 31-32
Countertransference, 126
Crime, 2, 8, 12,
    against women, 15

Criminal Justice Subcommittee Hearings (1984), 2

Death by homicide,
    black and white rates, 2
    of young black males, 2
Delinquency, juvenile, *see also* Measurements of delinquency
    genesis of, 4, 15n, 52-54
    as loners, 119
    penal facilities for, 79, 82, 90, 92-93, 96, 109, 110
    psychotherapy for, 123-126
    subcultures, 8
    theories of, 7-13
        psychoanalytic-clinical, 10-13
        psychological, 8-10
        sociological, 7-8
Delinquent behavior, 123
    genesis of, 4
Delinquents, black, 125
    psychotherapy denied, 123-126
    treatment strategies, 125-126
Dependency, 20, 24, 27, 48, 50, 77, 90, 111, 118
Depression, 25-26, 27, 48-49, 72, 83, 111-112, 123
Deprivation, 28, 38, 46, 50, 55, 95, 102, 116-117, 118
Determinism, social, 4-5
    arguments for and against, 4
    as explanation for crime, 4
Distress signal, 12, 55
Domination, 69-71

137